Satanic Ritual Abuse
Exposed

Satanic Ritual Abuse
Exposed

Recovery of a Christian Survivor

Katie

Revelation Gateway Publications, LLC

Satanic Ritual Abuse Exposed – Katie

Copyright © 2014

All rights reserved. No part of this book may be reproduced, stored in a retrieval system, or transmitted in any form or by any means – electronic, mechanical, photocopying, recording, or otherwise, without written permission from the publisher.

Scripture taken from the New King James Version®. Copyright © 1982 by Thomas Nelson, Inc. Used by permission. All rights reserved.

Scripture quotations marked (NIV) are taken from the Holy Bible, New International Version®, NIV®. Copyright © 1973, 1978, 1984, 2011 by Biblica, Inc.™ Used by permission of Zondervan. All rights reserved worldwide. www.zondervan.com The "NIV" and "New International Version" are trademarks registered in the United States Patent and Trademark Office by Biblica, Inc.™

Printed in the United States of America

First edition published 2013

Published by:

Revelation Gateway Publications, LLC
PO Box 342
Beaverton, OR 97075

Paperback ISBN: 978-1495466830

10 9 8 7 6 5 4 3 2 1

This book is available from www.amazon.com, Barnes & Noble, and through your local Christian bookstore.

Dedication

This book is dedicated to the millions of survivors of satanic ritual abuse (SRA) all over the world, who are looking for hope. It was written as a voice for the voiceless, declaring the love of God for restoration.

Contents

Dedication VII
Acknowledgements XI
Author's Note XIII
Introduction XV
Ch. 1: The Valley of Achor (Hosea 2:15) 1
Ch. 2: Pagoda for a Princess 7
Ch. 3: If You Could Only Read My Mind 15
Ch. 4: Run Away 19
Ch. 5: San Diego 29
Ch. 6: A Fugitive and Vagabond 35
Ch. 7: Denial of the Obvious 45
Ch. 8: The Ribbon Unravels 49
Ch. 9: New Beginnings 59
Ch. 10: Breakthrough 65
Ch. 11: Pandora's Box 79
Ch. 12: No Safe Place 85
Ch. 13: Rocky Mountains 95
Ch. 14: Living a Double Life 105
Ch. 15: Distant Places 109
Ch. 16: God Provides 115
Ch. 17: Amends 119
Ch. 18: Trusting with Fear and Trembling 127
Ch. 19: Mother 141
Ch. 20: Marionette Strings 155
Ch. 21: Bloodlines 165
Ch. 22: A New Millennium 167
Ch. 23: Divine Networking 175
Ch. 24: Why God? 181
Ch. 25: Connections 185
Ch. 26: Divine Appointments 191
Ch. 27: More to Remember 199
Ch. 28: Darkest Before the Dawn 205
Ch. 29: A Purpose for the Pain 211
About the Author 215

Acknowledgements

Thank you to my church family and friends who encouraged me to write this story and offered both their financial support and prayers. I would also like to express my appreciation, with deepest gratitude to each counselor and minister who patiently brought me through my past and into a new life of freedom. Most importantly, I praise God for all He has done to heal my broken heart and transform my life. May this work glorify Him.

Author's Note

The material in this book may be emotionally triggering for survivors of satanic ritual abuse and those who have experienced sexual abuse, mind control, or severe trauma. Please proceed with caution and the support of another person in the event this material might be disturbing. This book contains graphic, violent material that may be unsuitable for children.

Disclaimer: Names and locations have been changed throughout this book to protect those involved. Some literary license was taken in the recalling of specific conversations and events; however, this material was developed as accurately as possible. The author takes no responsibility for any similarity of this book to other people or events.

Introduction

During a California heat wave, on a blistering hot August evening in 1964, I burst forth from my mother's womb into the fiery depths of a living hell. I was born an Illuminati slave in a satanic cult, and as I looked back, I cursed my birth. I was held captive by mind control programming and trauma-induced amnesia, in bondage like a marionette on a string. My childhood was shattered into hundreds of tiny jigsaw puzzle pieces that were all jumbled together in the cloudiness of my mind. Seething, rushing torrents of pain swelled within me with each recovered memory. The inescapable horror of my childhood became a catalyst from which I was born again, into hands of living water.

Slowly and painstakingly I began piecing my life back together. Some pieces were easy to identify and slip into place, while others appeared incongruent and unwelcome as they floated up from the amnesia into my subconscious mind. My search for answers took me on a journey through a living nightmare but helped me find my way into the river of life. I am a ritual abuse survivor and this is my story. It is a chronicle of hope and deliverance – literal deliverance from evil.

Chapter 1

The Valley of Achor (Hosea 2:15)

———•———

My recovery began in a therapist's office where my husband Carl and I had gone for couples' counseling, for the first time. We entered the room a bit anxious. The counselor, Joanna, was warm and friendly, with short reddish blonde hair and silly socks. I liked her immediately.

We described to Joanna some of the challenges we were facing in our new marriage and our concern for Carl's two boys, then ten and twelve. Joanna listened intently and asked questions of us both before describing the dynamics of a codependent relationship. Then, to demonstrate an adult tantrum, she picked up a pillow from the couch and tossed it across the room.

Something snapped in me and I curled up in a ball on the floor, rocking back and forth, sobbing. After Joanna ushered Carl into the waiting room, she joined me on the floor.

The next thing I remembered is sitting in the passenger seat being driven home by Carl. He didn't say much, and just stared ahead at the road. I felt ashamed and afraid. My eldest half-brother had warned Carl not to marry me because he thought I was crazy, and I worried that maybe now Carl had proof about my brother being right. I feared that insanity festered at the back of my mind.

Joanna recommended I see her on an individual basis for a while, so I scheduled another appointment. In our next session we talked about what had happened previously, and Joanna gently asked, "Kathy, have you ever been sexually abused?"

I began to cry. "I don't know," I replied. "But I have been asked that question before."

As she continued to probe, it became painfully obvious that I remembered very little of my childhood and couldn't answer her questions with any certainty. Joanna felt there was a reason I couldn't remember and suggested we take some time to fill in the missing pieces.

She recommended taking a sheet of paper and creating a chronological timeline of things I could remember from my life. I thought that task would be relatively simple; but when I sat down to do it I was shocked at the gaps between years. Most of the paper was blank. I tried to stimulate my memory by going through my old baby book, looking for clues. My family wasn't big on pictures – most of the pages were empty except where I had filled them in myself. There were a handful of professional pictures taken when I was about six months old, and a black and white photograph of my mother holding me with the same exhausted look most new mothers have. There was also a tiny cutout of my father's face pasted on the page. Although he was forty years old, the look on his face was unmistakably mischievous, like that of an eight-year-old boy with a pocket full of firecrackers.

An old photo captured my attention. I stared at the image. I must have been about eighteen months old, wearing a little summer dress, running barefoot across the grass where ripe apricots lay scattered everywhere. I wondered what happened to that little girl.

I told Joanna everything I could remember about my childhood. I described the house we had in Campbell until the summer of my seventh birthday. It was an "Eichler" home, wrapped around a center atrium full of plants that could be seen from the kitchen and the living room. My mother's master bedroom had a sliding glass door that opened into the large backyard and pool. My father slept in a room beside mine at the end of the hall. I was my mother's only child, but my father had three grown-up children from his first marriage. They lived with us from time to time. John was the oldest, eighteen years my senior, then Jerry, and my sister Sara who was fourteen when I was born. During the mid-1960s, the Vietnam War was raging and both my brothers enlisted in the Navy and left for Southeast Asia. My sister moved from New Jersey to California to live with us, after being released from prison for heroin possession, and recovering from a severe automobile accident. I was only about six years old, but I recall her interest in magic and dark things like ravens and bats, which she wrote about in her poems. Strangely, she changed her name to Tanya.

Both my parents were heavy smokers and worked for Lockheed. My mother was a secretary and my father was a program manager. They worked long hours during the war years, and my father often traveled to Texas for long stretches at a time. I was left in the care of an alcoholic babysitter, Marion, from the time I was just a few weeks old until I was potty trained. I was placed in a preschool where I learned some basic French, ballet, and a great distaste for canned zucchini.

Saturday was my favorite day. My father would lie on the living room floor, leaning on one elbow and watching TV all day, while filling an ashtray. It was the only time it seemed he was around. So I would get my toys and play on the floor alongside him.

I remember when I first saw a John Wayne commercial warning people about the dangers of smoking. I panicked and begged my father to quit. "Please Daddy, I don't want you to die from smoking."

He just laughed and puffed out his chest and said, "Oh, horse feathers, Daddy is as healthy as an ox." But I could see that his teeth were rotten and his fingers were yellow from smoking four packs a day.

My parents fought fiercely whenever they were together. They would yell and curse in rapid-fire succession. At times mother would throw me in the car and take long drives while spouting profanities about my father. Mother could hold onto a grudge for dear life – her anger would burn like hot coals for days, smoldering under her breath.

As the only child, I looked to the adults in our home for attention, something mother seemed to begrudge me. I recall testing her limits from time to time, which usually ended with the sound of my mother's venomous words: "she's just doing it for attention," and a traumatic spanking from my father. She had the same attitude and verbal response to my frequent asthma attacks. She refused to comfort me and at times refused to provide medication, somehow believing even if she did I would only continue having the attacks.

My father, however, was quick to respond by finding my inhaler and sitting with me until the attack subsided. This often resulted in a fight between my parents over the treatment plan. I really missed my father when he wasn't home. He was my hero, up on a great big pedestal. In my eyes, he could do no wrong.

I was the only five-year-old to wear a purse to kindergarten, specifically to carry my asthma inhaler. My asthma was chronic and became increasingly worse as I grew older. Almost every day my lungs would seize and the world seemed to stop. I would struggle for air just like a drowning person unable to reach a life raft. Fear and panic would hit me sometimes, which only made the attacks worse. I learned to sit very still as I labored to breathe.

When all the other children were chasing about on the playground I would hear the teacher scold me, "Kathy, don't run it will cause an attack. Settle down!" I felt like I was handicapped. It irritated those responsible for me and made me feel different than the other children.

My father was always optimistic about my recovery. He had taken some premed classes at Princeton University and was convinced this ailment was a short-term issue. He assured me that someday I would outgrow the asthma and my chest would get bigger and the airways would get bigger and it would be easier for me to breathe. Even though his words gave me hope, they didn't bear fruit.

My fondest memories of my father were when he read to me. He bought the entire series of *Wizard of Oz* books by Frank Baum and read them to me on the nights he was home. His big bushy eyebrows would rise and fall with his voice to match the drama in the story. When he was done, he would lift the covers up over my shoulders and kiss me goodnight. That's when I knew he loved me.

Joanna asked me if I had any happy memories with my mother. I could only remember one. It was a Saturday and mom was playing "Herb Albert and the Tijuana Brass" on the stereo. She put her cigarette down and put me on her hip and danced with me. She spun me around and smiled. When she smiled her whole face lit up. It was the best moment we ever had.

CHAPTER 2

Pagoda for a Princess

In the summer of 1972, my parents bought an enormous home, designed like a Chinese pagoda, in the foothills of the Santa Cruz Mountains. The access road was a long curvy driveway that rose sharply, hugged the hillside, and leveled off as it forked to the right and ran alongside the house. At the corner of the house stood an eastern sun god poised to greet guests as they approached. At the apex of the house sat a life-size bronze Buddha, and at the far corner stood yet another cement god. In the hillside directly across from the western entrance was an ornate red door that opened to an old wine cellar. I remember being strictly forbidden to ever open that door. Atop the carriage house was a guesthouse, designed with a sloping roofline to compliment the oriental design of the main house.

The road beyond the guesthouse sloped down toward a couple of barns, stables, and a tack house. We owned the five acres remaining of the original estate. The estate was built by a California senator near the turn of the twentieth century, as a wedding gift for his wife. As a child, I remember exploring the rolling acres surrounding the house. There were several small buildings close to the main house, which was said to be where the senator's wife wrote her books. I was intrigued with the idea of being a writer and would sit in these shacks wondering what it must have been like for her.

There were old buggy trails that went from the house, deep

into the mountain, all the way to the beach in Santa Cruz. There were tales that the house was haunted – the senator's wife supposedly died in the large claw-foot bathtub on the main floor. I shuddered whenever I went in there. Opposite the tub was a walk-in linen closet so big that it had windows.

Ornate tiles, hand crafted by Chinese Cooley's, lined the walls of the living room. Enormous wooden pillars stood sentry at each end of the long living room, and the fireplace was large enough for me to stand inside. The house overlooked Silicon Valley, with an unobstructed, panoramic view. On a clear day you could see the Bay Bridge in San Francisco on the left, the airplane hangars at Moffett Field in the center, and the Pruneyard building in Campbell to the right. We sat on the roof of the third floor on the Fourth of July, and watched fireworks light the sky from every direction.

My mother took the master bedroom suite that was at the end of a long hallway on the eastern end of the main floor. The tiny sewing room, beside her room, was where my father slept and kept his belongings.

My bedroom was on the second floor. It had a nice little patio that joined with the guest bedroom, next to mine. A long, winding staircase led to the third floor, opening onto the crown jewel of the house – a large room with its windows offering breathtaking views and a warm quiet solace in the sun-drenched warmth of the top floor. Beneath the main floor were maid's quarters, gardener's quarters, another wine cellar, and a series of decks.

Soon after we moved into the house, my father bought a Jaguar XJ6, my mother bought evening gowns, and they headed to France for a vacation. I was left with my older half-siblings tasked with babysitting me and ensuring I was enrolled in the third grade. As a gift upon their return, my parents gave me two marionettes to play with, a dragon and a witch.

My parents took me to Hawaii during Christmas, for nearly

two weeks. Soon after that trip, I came home from school to find my father in the den looking at a book on the Philippines. "Daddy, what are you doing home so early?" I asked.

He smiled and said, "Well, I'm trying to decide which country to start my new business in – Australia or the Philippines."

"What?" I shrieked, "Are you leaving us?"

"Oh Kathy, daddy won't be gone for long, maybe a year."

"A year!" I screamed.

He drew me to himself and knelt down saying, "Daddy is going to make a million dollars and buy my little girl a pony. You can come visit me and maybe even go to school in another country. What do you think of that?"

"No Daddy, I don't want you to leave," I screamed as I ran to my room crying.

Just a short time later, my father was packing his bags. I remember my parents yelling back and forth through the house until a long black limousine glided up the driveway. My father kissed me, and promised to return soon. Then he climbed inside the big black car and it drove away. I just stood crying next to my mother, feeling terribly abandoned.

Within a week of his departure, the engine of dad's fancy new car froze, heralding the beginning of a long financial decline. Word came from the Philippines only a couple of times during the first year of dad's absence. He came home to visit once, and then was gone again. He was gone one year, then another.

I was told, "Daddy is in hiding, so he can't come home right now."

He was also unable to contribute financially, so mother worked full-time, but was still unable to pay the mortgage. We lived in a beautiful mansion, but ate rice and beans for dinner.

I was left alone in that big house all day long during the summer. I remembered feeling terribly alone and frightened. I sat for hours watching "Brady Bunch" reruns on TV until Watergate preempted every channel. Then I became a voracious reader.

One day the phone rang and a mysterious man asked about my sister Tanya. I told him she lived in our guesthouse, but was hardly ever home. Then he asked me what I was doing, and where we lived. Dutifully I gave him our address. Then he threatened to come over and rape me. I was so terrified and shaken-up that I called my mother at work. She scolded me for troubling her while she was busy. Hysterical, I ran up and down the stairs looking for a place to hide, expecting this evil man to arrive any moment.

Mother arranged to have the wife of dad's business associate look after me for the rest of the summer and after school. Her name was Karen and she had a little girl with cerebral palsy, named Betsy. Karen was an interesting woman. She spoke five languages and was the direct descendent of Spanish aristocracy. She had beautiful dark brown hair and eyes and a medium build.

I loved being at Karen's house. She taught me to cook, decorate, and tend the plants in the garden. When I had an asthma attack she would talk me through it, insisting I remain calm and take my medicine. Betsy was the little sister I never had but always wanted. Although I was five years her senior, I enjoyed playing with Betsy and watching Sesame Street together.

In the spring of 1974, Karen hosted an Easter party for Lockheed executives. There my mother met another man, named Joe. He was a very tall, thin man, several years older than my mother. He had steely-cold blue eyes and thin gray hair, tightly trimmed about his ears and neckline. He spoke fluent Portuguese and had a lengthy career at Lockheed. Instantly attracted to my mother, he started coming to our house every night, sometimes bringing flowers and occasionally a present for me. I began calling him Pappy.

It wasn't long before I was asked to sleep in my own bed so Pappy could sleep with mother. Alone at night, in my own room on the second floor, I was scared. No one could hear me when I had asthma attacks in the night – I was too far away. So I would labor to breathe, alone in the dark.

One evening my mother had a cocktail party and invited friends who knew my father from Lockheed and his business associates with Bestline products. They gave mother an update on his situation in the Philippines. At some point during the evening my mother discovered that my father was having an affair with a woman named Jean. After everyone left, mom stood in the living room crying in Pappy's arms about my father's unfaithfulness. It was total, bitter hypocrisy.

Mother cried a lot during that time. I was told as long as my father was in "hiding," there would be no communication. The Philippine president, Marcos, wanted to imprison my father, reportedly due to shady business dealings. We didn't know when or if he would return.

Life at home was tough, and so was the fourth grade. I wasn't well liked at school and was often teased and called a dog or "Kennel Ration Dog Chow." Looking back, I can only assume they saw me as weak, an easy target for humiliation, and easily angered when provoked.

I had only one friend who lived near our house; her name was Carolyn. Her family lived several miles up on top of the mountain. Every day after school, the bus would drop us off at the bottom of the hill and a member of Carolyn's family would always be there to pick her up and take her home. Usually I had to walk the half-mile up the hill to our house, but occasionally Carolyn's mom would give me a ride. We became close friends, and invited each other for sleepovers.

Her family was Christian and invited me to attend church with them one Sunday. It was the first and only time I had been to a Christian church. They took an interest in me and offered to pray for my family. The following Sunday, the nice people from the church came to our house to speak with my mother. I didn't hear what they said, but she flew into a rage and cursed them off of the property. I was so embarrassed. They didn't come around again.

However, I believe they prayed for me. I don't know who prayed, but I believe someone did. *Could those prayers have been the seeds that took root in my heart a decade later?* It inspires me to think that a simple prayer by an anonymous Christian saved my life.

My mother's older sister Virginia and her husband Bernie, from Detroit, came to visit us during the winter of the second year after dad was gone. They said they wanted to help my mom with her "responsibilities." I loved my aunt Ginny. She was soft and plump with orange curly hair and matching orange nail polish. She wore White Shoulders perfume every day. It permeated everything that was hers. I can still remember her fragrance wafting through the house, and her big warm hugs.

Aunt Ginny and Uncle Bernie were devout Catholics, and they went to the Catholic Church in town every Sunday without fail. They offered to take me too. I only remember going once, and I sat there and cried the entire service. I didn't know why I was crying, but I knew I didn't want to go back.

Aunt Ginny loved to sew and for Christmas she made me a red flannel nightgown with little white flowers around the collar. She took me shopping, taught me how to crochet, and baked cookies with me. She was the mom I always wanted.

In the evening, Aunt Ginny and Uncle Bernie would have cocktails with mom. The adults sat around for hours drinking and smoking. Uncle Bernie liked cigars and would lean back in his chair to blow smoke rings. Mom loved to play the organ and she would play old show tunes, like "Gypsy Rose Lee" or "Tie a Yellow Ribbon," while they sang the words. The smoke would get so thick in the living room that it would hang over them like a fog. If I complained, they sent me to my room. So I used to sit on the stairs, above the smoke, so I could breathe and watch the frivolity below. It was the only time I remember my mom being really happy.

During this time I had a curious fascination with World War II holocaust stories. I read *The Diary of Anne Frank* and similar stories I found in the library. Somehow, I deeply related to their pain, the torture they suffered, and their imprisonment.

When I was ten, our house was put up for sale and divorce proceedings began between my parents. Aunt Virginia and Uncle Bernie returned to Michigan and it seemed my world turned upside down. I felt like a lost little girl.

Mother sold our house during the summer of 1975, tearfully exclaiming that she narrowly avoided foreclosure. She dragged the bedroom furniture I got for my seventh birthday out to the driveway and held a garage sale. She said there wasn't enough room for it in our new house.

Before I knew it, all the materialistic trappings of prosperity were washed away along with every item that belonged to my father. His cars, clothes, furniture, cuff links – all were gone.

"Can't we wait for daddy to get back?" I screamed at mother.

I cried for weeks. I didn't want to move. I waited for him three years, but he didn't come home.

Mother took our dogs to the pound, despite my protests. Three days later, with tears in her eyes, she brought them back before they were euthanized. She found good homes for them before we moved, but I was grief-stricken. I couldn't imagine what mother was going through or the strength it took for her to do what she did. I was simply oblivious.

We moved into a small house in Cupertino with Pappy. Six months later we moved into a condominium they bought in Mountain View. Three days after my mother's divorce from my father was final, Pappy married my mother.

The move to Mountain View required me to be transferred to a new school for sixth grade. This was a dramatic shift for me socially. It was like going from a private school in Beverly

Hills to a public school in the Watts district of LA. I didn't fit in from the very beginning, and the other children didn't hesitate to let me know. They teased me mercilessly and occasionally threw food. A fourth-grader chased me home one day, threatening to beat me up.

On picture day, I looked sick, weak, and gaunt with really bad hair; it's the worst picture of me ever taken. I was embarrassed to show it to mother and was mortified to later discover she had sent one to father, in the Philippines.

My health continued to decline that year until it was particularly serious. I was feeling very ill one morning, but my mother insisted I go to school. By the end of the day I was unable to breathe and felt too weak to walk home. I sat on the bench in the schoolyard hoping to catch my breath. Kids mocked and jeered as they walked past. I finally persuaded myself to walk the few blocks necessary to get home for safety. Mother got home a few hours later and I begged her to take me to the doctor, but the doctor's office was closed by then. Mother grumbled about the hours of waiting in the emergency room, but finally agreed to take me in. When we got there my lips and nails were blue. I was diagnosed with pneumonia and was immediately admitted to the hospital. The doctor scolded my mother and she left the hospital in tears. Later that night I was transferred to the pediatric unit, still unable to breathe.

I remember a nurse telling me, "You hold on child, you can make it." She looked me straight in the eye and firmly said, "Don't you give up now."

I wondered, "How does she know I feel like dying? How does she know I don't think I *can* hang on?"

I didn't realize this valuable truth then, but *to breathe is to take in life.*

Chapter 3

If You Could Only Read My Mind

I saw Joanna on a weekly basis as I filled in the years of my life that I could remember. I complained about my stepsons, my husband, our new baby, finances, and insomnia.

She asked me if I had trouble sleeping at other times in my life. I told her there was a time in sixth grade, right after my mother married Pappy, when I was afraid to sleep at night because fear plagued me. At the age of eleven, I would lay there in the dark, afraid and tormented, sometimes becoming hysterical without any explanation. I didn't know what I was afraid of or why I was crying. I tossed and turned, sobbing in my bed. I didn't know what was wrong with me, but I did know mother was becoming increasingly exasperated because I was making so much noise every night.

She would yell, "Just close your eyes and go to sleep!"

It didn't help at all. I felt very unsafe and vulnerable.

My mother found me sitting at the dining room table one night, wearing her big, pink robe. She put her arms around me and asked gently, "Kathy, why are you crying?"

I looked at her and said, "Momma I don't know why. I wish I knew. If you could only read my mind, maybe you could help me," I said, imploring her.

"If I could help you honey I would," she replied. Then she patted me on the head and went back to bed.

The night terrors and insomnia continued for more than a year, along with chronic bladder infections. I remember Karen coming to visit us and my mother complaining to her about it. I felt embarrassed and ashamed. Mother finally resorted to forcing me to take naps. When I refused, she threatened me, saying, "If you don't stop this right now I am going to take you to see a psychiatrist."

Fear of a psychiatrist was somehow worse than my fears at night, so I stole Valium from her bathroom and forced myself to be quiet in my room. She continued to refill the prescription thinking Pappy was taking the pills.

Joanna asked me if the insomnia felt the same now, as it did then.

"Yes," I replied. "I wish I could explain it." But for some reason the insomnia dissipated after I took a trip to New Mexico just before I turned twelve.

That summer, mother sent me to stay with Karen and Betsy. They had moved into an old ranch in New Mexico with Karen's new husband Bob and his kids. It was a fantastic journey. I was so excited to see Karen and Betsy again. The drive from the airport to the ranch was a long one in a car packed with kids, but we sang and had a good time. The ranch was isolated in the mountains, rustic and very rugged. Almost every afternoon it would rain for a while, and I recall seeing wild horses running by.

We took a trip to town every week for supplies. On a hot summer day, during our weekly visit to town, we were driving back to the ranch when my lungs seized violently. I was in the front seat of the station wagon with Karen. She immediately pulled over and I got out of the car, gasping for breath.

Karen asked, "Kathy, do you need a doctor?" I couldn't

breathe and I couldn't speak. I shook my head as if to say yes and passed out.

I woke up in a hospital bed, several hours later. A doctor came in, and I recall his words precisely.

He said, "You're awake? We didn't think you would ever wake up. You gave us all a good scare."

Over thirty years after this event I recovered this trauma memory. I could see myself on an emergency room table from where I was floating up near the ceiling.

I heard, "She's blue, get the oxygen."

I could see the medical personnel frantically working over my body.

Then I heard the words "She's gone," and then I saw the doctor look up at the clock.

From my perch in the corner, I saw Jesus come into the room and place his hand over my heart. He turned and looked up at me and said, "It's not your time yet." Slowly the color returned to my face.

Karen came into the room with tear-stained cheeks and hugged me. "We almost lost you," she said. "You turned blue!" she said, crying. "If we hadn't been in town so close to the hospital…"

I couldn't move – every limb in my body felt like it weighed a hundred pounds. The realization that I almost died was sinking in, and I too started crying.

Karen said, "Your mother is on her way from California. She will be here to get you tomorrow. The doctor says you need to go home but you mustn't travel alone. They are going to let us take you back to the ranch tonight, but you will fly home in the morning."

I felt so weak and sad. The next morning Karen made homemade donuts on the wood-burning stove and then packed the station wagon for the long drive to the airport. I was happy to see my mother, but she wasn't very happy to see me. She was angry and let me have it as soon as we returned home.

"How could you pull a stunt like this?" She said, "You were just homesick and had to get attention, didn't you? I have used up all of my vacation time and my sick leave to take care of you. The plane ticket cost more than two hundred dollars. I hope you are satisfied," she hissed.

"Mama, no," I cried. "It wasn't like that at all. I'm so sorry."

Joanna listened intently when I told her the things I remembered. Then she said, "Kathy, kids don't ask to be sick. It wasn't your fault."

I started crying and twisted the wad of Kleenex in my hand. Our hour seemed to finish so quickly.

Chapter 4

Run Away

I was twelve years old when my father returned from the Philippines. I remember the day well. After the phone call, Pappy and I were both digging in mom's bathroom for the bottle of little yellow Valium pills. Mother was quite calm about seeing her ex-husband. We were a mess.

There was a knock on the door and in walked a very thin man I barely recognized as my father. He had lost sixty pounds during the four years he was gone and had aged dramatically. His hair had thinned and grayed, and his face was worn from sun and great distress.

He smiled a big toothless grin and exclaimed, "Kathy, how you've grown!" He wrapped his arms around me as I stood there in a state of shock.

Mother, Pappy, my father, and I assembled together on the gold L-shaped couch in the living room. We listened intently as dad told us the story of his escape from the Philippines. His voice broke with emotion and I watched his face animate as he described the perils of his adventure.

"For a year or so I stayed with Ding in Manila," he said. "Ding had eight children. They were good people," he mumbled. "I lived from place to place to stay hidden. Jean was the one who insisted I go into hiding. She warned me that a Philippine jail was no place for an American. She believed it would be a death sentence. Jean saved my life," he said. "I used to meet her at the park and she would bring me food, pocket money, cigarettes, and laundered clothes."

A look of longing crossed his face and I knew he loved her.

"During holy week in the Philippines everything shuts down for celebration and the military is less vigilant. That's when I planned my escape," he explained. "Jean gave me a pouch full of diamonds to use for bribing my way through any security posts and to cover travel expenses. I used a little five-horsepower dingy to travel from Manila to Hong Kong with a guide. It took ten days. We ran out of food and water in a shark-infested ocean." He shook his head and sighed. "I wasn't sure we would make it. But once in Hong Kong, I bought a plane ticket to San Francisco and then John picked me up at the airport yesterday. I'm still feeling pretty weak."

Mom and Pappy expressed concern for dad's health and wished him well as he left that day. Dad's return was such a shock to me. Repressed rage boiled inside me, but I had no idea how to cope with my feelings. I couldn't be angry around my mother without earning quick reprisal. So I stuffed my feelings with food.

When my mother said "You're getting fat," I stopped eating and became anorexic. I starved myself for days, and then I binged until I couldn't hold any more. At one point I was so thin I can remember lying in the bathtub feeling all of my bones. Pappy noticed, but my mother didn't.

My stepfather was better to me than my biological father, but when my mother went off to one of her "meetings," Pappy took the opportunity to have sex with me. It was our dirty little secret that took me twenty-five years to remember.

Dad got on his feet quickly. He stayed with my half-brother John until he secured a job selling mobile homes. Then he rented one for himself and his new bride, Jean. Whenever I went to visit he spoke of her with deep longing. It took him a year to get her visa released so she could come to America to be with him. I don't know when or where they married. He was very private about that subject and he assumed correctly that I wouldn't understand.

My father insisted on seeing me after school at least once a week. But I didn't want to see him. Inside tumbled a powerful mixture of rage, resentment, and the pain of abandonment. As a good little girl, raised in a highly dysfunctional family, I didn't know what to do with those feelings. I do remember thinking "How *dare* he come back into my life and expect everything to be the same after four years." But I don't think I ever shared those words with him. Instead I avoided his calls and stood him up occasionally.

That summer I developed an insatiable interest in boys. My friend KC started teasing me about being a virgin and convinced me I was the only virgin left. One night we went out driving with a group of older boys from the high school. I was in the backseat of the station wagon with a young man named David. He was gorgeous with thick blond curls and a deep golden California tan. He expressed quite an interest in me. Starved for attention and affection, I invited him over the next day when my parents were at work and consented to having sex. He kept saying, "I can't believe you're a virgin, where did you learn to do that?" I didn't know and started crying. I never saw him again.

Later KC said, "You believed me when I said those things? I didn't think you would really do it. You are so gullible," she squealed. "Tell me everything."

It turned out she was still a virgin. But once that line had been crossed, I had no boundaries and consented to having sex with anyone who expressed an interest.

I spent most of the summer in the pool or in the condominium clubhouse playing billiards with the boys. When my mother discovered my whereabouts she began to clamp down and restrict my activities. My resentment toward her began to build. I wanted to scream at her, "Where were you all those years when I needed you most?" The older I got, the more I chaffed against her authority.

My father tried to buy my affection with jewelry and gifts, but I held onto my grudge with vengeance. In eighth grade, he picked me up after school with a girlfriend of mine and asked us what we wanted to do. We wanted cash and a ride to the mall for make-up. He obliged us and spent over a hundred dollars on me at the cosmetics counter.

My mother was furious when she found out. "You are only thirteen years old and no daughter of mine is going to wear make-up like a tramp," she screamed.

She forced me to go to the store with her to return it all and made a loud scene, embarrassing me beyond reason. I hated her for it.

I have very little memory of the summer before high school, but I do remember my freshman year. That's when I met Monique. She and her family had just moved to Silicon Valley from San Diego. She was petite and dark, a lovely mixture of French and Mexican. Her gorgeous, long black hair tumbled about her shoulders and her sporty athletic build brought a lot of attention from the boys. I was tall, blonde, and sickly looking in high school, her exact opposite.

We had algebra and PE classes together. Neither of us was very good at algebra. I laugh thinking about the time our teacher caught us counting ceiling tiles when we should have been taking notes.

Then he asked, "Well, how many tiles are there?"

In stereo we gave him an exact number. The next semester we were put in remedial math.

Monique shined like an Olympic athlete in PE. The teacher asked her to coach the class during gymnastics season because she was so skillful. I remember her lovingly teasing me because I was awkward and clumsy.

"Come on KK," that's what she used to call me, "You can do it!"

Usually I fell on my butt, which was good for a hearty laugh at my expense. We were like cookies and milk together.

The same year I set my sights on a young man named Jay. He was two years my senior; tall, trim, and blond, with a strong spiritual and philosophical bent to his personality. At the time we met he was dating someone else, but that didn't discourage me. I waited patiently, anticipating their inevitable break-up.

Jay's best friend Jim liked Monique, and it wasn't long before the four of us were double dating. On the week-ends mom and Pappy left me home alone while they set up their new retirement home in Clear Lake, a few hours away. I was all too happy to have the condo to myself so I could invite my friends over and listen to "Earth, Wind & Fire" albums, party, and have sex. I fell head over heels in love with Jay. We committed to a monogamous relationship and relished every opportunity to sunbathe or camp in the hills, neck between classes, or go to a concert together.

In June of 1979, my mother and I had a fight. It had been building up for quite some time, but I don't remember the specifics. I quickly packed a few things in a bag and left. I was fourteen years old.

My mother chased me down the hall in her pink bathrobe yelling, "Kathy you come back here."

I turned to look at her, but kept going. I ran across the street to the 7-Eleven to use the pay phone. I called Jay, hysterical. He immediately drove to the store to pick me up. His mother agreed to let me stay with them for a few days, as long as we had separate bedrooms and I agreed to help with housework.

Jay's mom was a neat lady. She reminded me a little of my Aunt Ginny. She had strawberry blond hair pinned up with big curls and an obvious affinity for wine. Clearly, she loved her son very much and doted on him hand and foot.

"No wonder he is so spoiled," I remember thinking as I vacuumed their living room.

The first night away from home I slept in Jay's room and cried myself to sleep. Jay snuck in and tried to comfort me, but it was no use. After a few days I was concerned that I was wearing out my welcome, so I accepted the invitation from Monique's parents to take me in.

Monique's dad was a strikingly handsome man with the charisma of a politician. Her mom was petite, blonde, and beautiful, with a delightful French accent and a laugh that would light up the room. They insisted I call my mother to tell her I was all right. This I did with trepidation.

"Kathy, you get home right now," my mother demanded. "I'm not fooling around anymore. It's been a week and I want you home within an hour, or I will call the police."

Very calmly I said, "Go ahead and call the police, I'm not coming home."

Monique's father overheard the conversation and left the house a few minutes later with his briefcase. Monique and I sat in their living room and waited for the police to knock on the door. My stomach was in my throat and I had no idea what to expect, but I was resolute about my decision. A short time later Monique's father returned and said he had spoken with my mother. "Don't worry," he said, "the police wouldn't be coming."

He had a PhD in psychology and a strong sense that returning home wasn't the best thing for me. Monique's family invited me to stay with them until I could make other arrangements.

In the evening Monique and her family enjoyed their meal and sat around talking for hours. Her dad asked me lots of questions, things I had never considered before. Then he described my relationship with my mother as "plastic." His words really stuck with me. One of the things I admired about Monique was the fact that she was straightforward and honest with me like her father.

From Monique's home I moved into the mountains to live with my half-brother Jerry and his wife Linda. Jay came every weekend to see me. After several weeks Jerry rented a little trailer in town for us to live in. It was the very first place I could call my own. It was tiny and cramped, but sufficient for our needs.

To support myself I needed to work. So I lied about my age and got my first job at the local A&W restaurant for two dollars an hour. After two weeks on the job I brought home fifty dollars. I felt discouraged, and quit.

During this time my dad and his new wife Jean came to visit. When they realized Jay and I were living together they urged us to get married.

Without hesitation I screamed, "No way! I'm only fourteen!"

Needless to say they didn't stay long to visit.

After they left, Jay tenderly said, "I'll marry you Kathy if that's what you want."

Then we made love and the rubber broke. I recall several worrisome weeks before my cycle began and arrested our fear of pregnancy.

Reality roared at Jay and I like a freight train at full speed. It was the end of August, I had just turned fifteen and school was about to begin again. Jay wanted to return home to his parents so he could finish his senior year at the high school where we met. Without a better solution, I moved back in with my mother and Pappy.

Mother seemed happy to have me home. But I considered

it a short-term visit and kept all of my belongings in boxes. I returned to high school for my sophomore year and got a job as a waitress at a restaurant in Palo Alto. After school I took the bus to the restaurant, worked until 11:00 p.m., then took the bus home with an apron full of change. I did homework at dawn and made it to school by 8:00 a.m. Over the course of a couple of months I saved enough money to buy a moped to get back and forth between work and school. When my mother discovered I was saving money to get an apartment and planned to leave again, she promptly threw me out.

I had nowhere else to go, so I called my father. He had a two-bedroom apartment in Sunnyvale for his new wife Jean and their adopted daughter, Lori, from the Philippines.

The apartment was small and I had no privacy sharing a bedroom with Lori. She was only twelve years old and was learning English. She didn't seem to mind having me there, but I was restless and unhappy. I was gone most of the time anyway so I tried to make the best of the situation.

School was tough for me. Rather than focusing on grades, I was thinking about the apartment I wanted and where I could get a better job. Unable to manage traditional classes, I decided to join an alternative learning program at the school where there was less stress and more support. During that time, Jay and I broke up. I was utterly devastated.

I became suicidal and seriously ill again. One morning my father found me unconscious, collapsed on the kitchen floor with a high fever and having convulsions.

Two weeks from the end of my sophomore year I wanted to quit school. I was depressed and hopeless; and felt like I just couldn't go on. One of my instructors talked me into taking the California State Proficiency Exam and urged me to finish the last two weeks of school. Gratefully I followed his advice, which qualified me for college. I passed the exam and left high school, but regretted that I wouldn't be going to prom and graduating with the class of 1982.

After I left school, my father offered to help me get my own studio apartment. It wasn't just his sense of charity. I was disrupting life with his new wife and daughter, and caused problems by staying out late or not coming home at all. If he locked the front door before I came home, he found me curled up asleep on the welcome mat in the morning.

He rented a studio for me in Mountain View, close to my job. I was ecstatic to have my own place. I fixed it up and invited friends over. But truthfully I was lonely and frightened, especially at night.

I often woke having had nightmares, and paced the room until morning. Funny how some dreams just stick with you. I recall one particularly upsetting dream about a man dressed as Uncle Sam coming through my window to hurt me. Why would I be afraid of the government?

To quench my fears I binged on food and alcohol. That summer my half-brother Jerry and his wife Linda invited me to Disneyland for a family vacation with Tanya, her husband, and their kids. I jumped at the invitation; it was something I always wanted to do. We traveled in their station wagon, packed to the gills with kids, luggage, and snacks, and arrived eight hours later.

At the gates to the Magical Kingdom I met Jim. He was a hippie, with long brown hair, a soft raspy voice, and beautiful brown eyes. We got to know each other standing in long lines for rides and screaming down roller coasters. We parted that night and promised to meet at the park again in the morning. He greeted me the next day with a kiss and a poem. I was in love. At the end of the day, he took the bus south to San Diego and I went north with my family. I remember sitting in the back seat with my nieces, smelling pot smoke drifting from the front, and crying all the way home.

Monique and I remained friends, though we didn't see each other as often as we did when we were at school together. She also took the proficiency exam and left high school when I did. She too started having problems at home and came over one day to admire my apartment.

"Hey Monique," I said, "How about you moving in with me? Wouldn't it be fun?"

She shook her head. "My dad told me if I ever ran away I couldn't come back. That would be it. I'm not sure I'm ready to make that decision," she said. "Besides, this place is kind of small."

"Well, what do you want to do?" I asked her.

She replied, "I want to move back to San Diego."

"Really? I'd love to go to San Diego with you. Monique I have to tell you about this guy I met down there..."

Chapter 5

San Diego

Monique and I packed our suitcases and had bus tickets to San Diego within days of our discussion. It was a twelve-hour bus ride with a transfer in downtown LA. Monique and I were nervously standing in the bus terminal waiting for the next bus to arrive. Monique pulled a cigarette out of her purse and offered me one. "Here, it will calm you down," she said.

I coughed and gagged. "This isn't calming me down," I replied.

"Oh hush up, don't be such a baby," she said. "Come on, there's our ride."

We scrambled onto the bus and two hours later pulled into the station in San Diego. I was wide-eyed as I looked around. There were beautiful women propositioning the sailors and two of them approached us. Pinkie and Gigi asked if we had a place to stay or if we would like to join them. I was dumbfounded and speechless.

Monique spoke up, "No thanks, we have plans." She grabbed my arm and said, "Don't be stupid KK, they're prostitutes. You don't want to be a prostitute, do you?"

I shook my head.

Monique had friends in Mission Beach. She called from a pay phone and asked if we could crash there for a while. We took the city transit in that direction and stopped for pizza when we reached our destination. From there we found the address where we had planned to stay for the night. Then I called Jim.

"Tell me where to find you and I'll meet you in the morning," he said.

The next morning, Jim and I walked along the beautiful shores of Mission Beach hand-in-hand and made plans to be together.

He looked right through me and said, "I love you babe." Then we kissed.

The house where we were staying was filled with college students and a couple engaged to be married. Monique and I had only been there a couple of days when she seduced the groom-to-be into having sex with her, and his fiancé threw us out.

We landed in an old section of San Diego called North Park. There we pooled our resources and rented an apartment from an elderly lady. It was a nice two-bedroom unit with orange shag carpet. A few blocks away I got a job in the health food store as a clerk, selling vitamins, herbs, and bulk foods. Monique found a position at an expensive clothing store downtown. We picked up a third roommate, Lisa, to help cover expenses. Lisa was a runaway too.

Jim lived with his parents in Chula Vista, seven miles from the Mexican border. He was on probation for being in the wrong place, with the wrong people, when a crime was committed. By law he had to stay with his mother, but he took a job in North Park to be near me. Jim worked at the bakery down the street, and would come over after work, covered in flour.

For my sixteenth birthday my father drove down from San Jose and brought us a trailer full of furniture from Monique's parents and the remaining items left from my studio apartment. He took Jim and me out for dinner and pointedly asked our intentions for the future. We had none. Tension hung heavy between us and we were all very uncomfortable.

The next day my father drove me over to San Diego Community College and insisted I enroll in classes for the fall term.

The clerk looked at me and said, "I think you are one of the youngest students we have ever had here."

When my father returned to San Jose I tossed the college forms in the trash and went back to work.

I think it was October when Jim let me know his mother was sending him to Oklahoma to live with his grandmother. He had no choice but to comply because of his probation. I was heartbroken and devastated to the extent that I couldn't maintain my job. I got another one, but was promptly fired. I distinctly remember walking home that day and stopping at a freeway overpass. I stood there contemplating a jump when Monique came by on a bicycle.

"KK what are you doing here?" she asked gently. "Come away from there."

I turned and looked at her.

"Kathy, no. You can't do this. Come home with me."

She walked the rest of the way back to the apartment with me. She produced a quart of rum and a six-pack of Diet Coke and we proceeded to get loaded.

Monique said, "KK, you remember those beautiful women we saw at the Greyhound station when we first got here?"

"Yeah."

"Guess what?" she giggled. "Those weren't women."

"What?" I exclaimed, jaw gapping. "How do you know that?"

"They came into the store the other day. They are transvestites."

"No way," I shrieked. We laughed and rolled on the floor. By morning we were both throwing up, and were sick for two days.

Monique decided she wanted to go back home to San Jose. We had signed a six-month lease on the apartment and there was still a month or more to go on it.

"You can't just leave me here Monique," I complained.

"Come with me then," she said. "I'll find a place for us."

"No, we are responsible for this lease, I can't just leave."

"So what if we break the lease," she replied, "It's no big deal. Just come back with me."

I insisted on staying, and Monique left. By that time Lisa was gone too. Unable to get a job and unable to pay the rent, I just sat in the empty apartment alone. I ran out of food quickly, and went without eating for several days. I remember going to Balboa Park to walk around and break up the long days. I loved to watch people go by or simply to draw or scribble in my journal under the fragrant eucalyptus trees. I met a young man there who took me home with him to have Thanksgiving dinner with his family.

His mama looked at me and said, "Child, you don't look too undernourished to me. My boy says you haven't eaten in a while, is that true?"

"Yes ma'am," I replied.

They fed me well and I went back to the apartment. My father called that night and asked how I was doing. I burst into tears. "Daddy, Monique left, Jim went to Oklahoma, and Lisa moved out. I'm here all alone, I don't have a job, and I ran out of food."

The next day my father returned to San Diego with a trailer for the furniture and brought me back to San Jose. I didn't know what to say to him on the long drive home. So I curled up in a little ball on the floor in the front seat of his car and slept the entire trip home.

When we reached San Jose my father said, "Kathy, you are going to live with your brother John. You are going back to school and you are going to pull your life together. Your housing is conditional upon education. John and Kimberly are willing to keep you, but you must go back to school."

"Okay," I agreed with a pout.

On my first day back in town I was offered a job at a nearby health food store, within walking distance from John's house. Then dad took me to the junior college in Gilroy and enrolled me in classes for the winter term.

John and his wife Kimberly were wonderful to me. They gave me my own room, fed me, and listened to the troubles of my heart. Kimberly even taught me how to drive, and my father helped me buy my first car. It was a little red 1968 VW bug, with dual exhaust and beautiful white leather interior. I complied with their demands and took a full load of classes, including a course on death and dying.

Kimberly asked, "Why would you take a course on death and dying? That sounds so morbid."

To which I replied, "You might think this is strange, but I have the feeling dad is going to die and I just want to be prepared to handle it when the time comes."

Kimberly was really close to my dad so this didn't settle well with her. "You're right," she said. "That is strange."

Chapter 6

A Fugitive and Vagabond

I met Robert in art history class at the college. He too left high school when he was young, and his mother insisted he too go back to school. We had a lot in common and became drinking buddies, close friends, lovers, and later roommates. I rented a little shack in Gilroy, not far from the college. Robert, his sister, and her little boy all moved in with me. I finished the term on the Dean's List, but didn't enroll for additional classes. At some point, I quit my job. We sat around the shack all day doing amphetamines and drinking Gallo wine by the gallon. The stove didn't work, so we used "Polly Perk," a little electric hot water pot, to make ramen noodles. On my seventeenth birthday, I remember doing "mushrooms in the hills," and later LSD at a "Day on the Green" concert.

That time of my life is really quite a blur. But I remember my dad moving me in with him at his new house in San Jose that year. Again, he insisted I reenroll in school, but this time saying, "Kathy you need to get off the drugs."

"How do you know I'm doing drugs?" I snapped back at him.

"Never mind, I just know," he said resolutely.

"Whatever," I replied sarcastically under my breath.

I took another job at a health food store and enrolled at West Valley Jr. College. Almost every night after school I drove over to Robert's dad's house to drink and party with him. One night I drank so much wine that I drove my car into a parked vehicle, woke up, and proceeded to drive around the block. When I got out of the car I realized I was naked. Like a crazy person, I went running down the street screaming. Robert heard the commotion outside and brought me back in the house to spend the night.

The next day I lied to my dad about the car. "You know, the brakes on that thing are terrible and I hit a tree," I told him with a straight face.

He was really mad. "I knew something like this would happen. **** it!" he said. Then he made arrangements to have the front end fixed and didn't bring it up again.

Jean was not happy with me either. "You treat dis house like hotel," she yelled. "You no respect your fader and me."

As she was yelling, I handed her my dirty dinner plate and said, "Here, clean this up too."

That was it. She grabbed a butcher knife and lunged for me. My father grabbed Jean and screamed at me to get out of the house. I peeled away in my car and headed to Robert's dad's house.

The next day at school dad met me in the cafeteria during lunch. "What are *you* doing here?" I asked him.

"Kathy, we have to talk," he said, taking a seat. "You can't stay with us anymore. Jean is furious. She doesn't let go of things like this easily, so you are going to have to find another place to live."

It must have pained him terribly to say that to me. But I was narcissistic and had little compassion for other people. I was enmeshed in my own drama and pain.

I rented a little cabin in the hills near Boulder Creek. It was a summer cabin with no heat and lots of moisture in the wintertime, but it was cheap. I recruited a roommate from work and we slept on the floor in front of the fireplace to keep warm. All my books molded and it was miserably uncomfortable there. The commute up and down the mountain every day to work and school was tedious as well. But I enrolled for a second semester at the college and was attempting to get my life on track.

Then I derailed over a single phone call. It was Valentine's Day, 1982. I was lonely and depressed, so I called Jim at his grandmother's in Oklahoma.

His soft raspy voice said, "I miss you babe, I wish you were here."

I dropped everything to go. My friend Stacy said she wanted to come with me too. So we dropped all our classes, packed my VW bug and headed for Oklahoma. On the way we stopped in New Mexico to visit Karen and Betsy. Then off again we went to Oklahoma City. We were driving my little car hard and fast as we came through a little town aptly named Corn. There the engine froze and we were stuck on the side of the road, about 100 miles from our destination. Stacy and I wasted no time putting our thumbs out to hitch a ride. Soon enough a truck with a couple of cowboys picked us up and took us to the nearest cheap motel to party for the night.

The next day Jim met me with his grandmother's station wagon and towed my little red bug behind it all the way into town. I had never been to Oklahoma City, so everything about it was new to me. Nana's house was brick with a big front room window and humble decor. Jim lived there with his Uncle Bob, Bob's little girl Leanne, and Jim's great aunt. There wasn't much room for Stacy and me, but we were welcome to sleep on the living room floor.

It had been well over a year since I'd seen Jim, but I thought that flame was still burning strong. Whenever I was near him I just melted in his arms. He seemed genuinely glad to see me.

We went out for dinner that night with Nana. I liked her

instantly. She was warm and genuine with a loving angelic quality about her.

"What are you running from child?" she asked me directly.

"Me? I'm not running," I replied.

She smiled knowingly. "Oh, I think you are. Maybe you just don't know it yet. But you are running just the same."

I excused myself from the table feeling rather weak, and went to the ladies room. They later found me there, passed out on the floor. Nana insisted I go to the hospital for tests. It turned out to be something hormonal.

I called my dad and informed him there was a problem with the car engine.

"Well, where are you?" he asked.

"Umm, you're not going to like this," I stammered, "I'm in Oklahoma City."

The line went silent on the other end for a moment. Then I knew for sure he was mad.

"What on earth are you doing in Oklahoma City?" he demanded.

"I came out here to be with Jim," I replied.

Somehow my father tolerated my escapades and supported me through them as best he could. He told me to tow the car to a shop and he would make arrangements to get it fixed under warranty. As long as the car was in the shop, I was told to stay put – even if it took weeks. I quickly got a job, then we rented a trashy apartment that we fondly called the "Roach Motel." Never in my life had I ever seen cockroaches like we had there. They were big, black ugly critters that scared me at night whenever I turned the lights on. We scraped and borrowed, and before long Stacy and I pulled our little apartment together with some used furnishings and hand-me-down linens.

I was working in a little health food store in the mall for a sweet little Christian woman named Doris. She must have been in her late seventies and for some reason she could see right through me. One night as we were closing the store she said to me, "Could you use a little extra food at your place? I think it's time to clean out this old freezer."

She loaded two sacks full of groceries and sent me home with them.

We weren't living in the apartment long before Jim started coming home later and later at night. A few times he came home so drunk he wet his pants and passed out. Tension rose between us and I started nagging and complaining. Then one day I found the journal I had given him for his birthday. It had only one entry in it, about another woman.

When we finally talked about it, Jim told me the truth. He really hadn't expected me to come back into his life and he wasn't ready for a commitment.

"I will always love you Kathy, but I just can't meet your expectations," he confessed.

The song "Angie" was playing on the car radio when we decided to split up. I was heartbroken and furious. Jim went back to Nana's house; Stacy and I remained in the apartment.

One evening Tony, Stacy's boyfriend, came over looking for her, with a fist full of money.

"She's not here," I said, as he plopped down on the bed and started counting.

My eyes gapped and my mouth opened wide, "Tony, where did you get all that money?"

He leaned back, smiling as he counted his wad. "I sold my mama's rings."

"What?" I exclaimed.

"Hush," he said. "You better keep your mouth shut." When he finished counting, he shoved the bills in his pocket, kissed me on the cheek, and left. A short time later his mama came to the door with a shotgun.

"Where is he?" she demanded, barging through the door.

I was home alone. Terrified, she backed me up against the wall and screamed in my face, "Where's Tony?"

"I don't know," I answered.

"Was he here?" she barked, poking her head into each of the rooms.

"Yes," I confessed.

"He stole my jewelry and I want it back," she bellowed.

"I know," I said softly, "I saw the money."

"You did?" She queried with a turn of her head and a sly smile.

"Uh huh," I answered.

"Good. Don't you go nowhere now," she threatened. "I'll have the police follow up with you."

She promptly lowered the shotgun and left. I slumped to the floor and started bawling. I didn't know what to do or where to go. So I called Jim at Nana's.

"A terrible thing has happened. I don't know what to do," I cried.

"Just come over here," he suggested, "we'll talk about it."

So I walked to Nana's house. When I got there the house was full of people watching MTV and smoking. Tony was there too.

Nearly hysterical I said, "Tony, your mama came to the apartment looking for you with a shotgun."

"What did you tell her?" he demanded.

"I told her I saw the money."

"You WHAT?" he screamed along with a long string of profanity. Tony drew right up close to me and snarled through his teeth, "All I can tell you girl is you better get out of this town and I mean NOW before you get hurt."

I was shaking and crying. Jim just shook his head with disapproval at me and put out his smoke.

"We don't turn on folks like that here," he said. "You never did belong."

"I can't leave yet. My car is still in the shop and I don't have any money until I get paid next week."

"Well, you can't go back to the apartment. You are going to have to stay here for a little while and you will have to quit that job."

Once again Nana took me in. I cleaned her place from top to bottom. I didn't know how else to repay her. Jim was cool and distant.

Finally the day came when the car was finished. Jim agreed to meet me at the bar to say our goodbyes. On the way to the bar I was pulled over for speeding. Frustrated and upset I somehow wrapped the strap of my purse around the steering column and swerved as I was pulling over. The officer didn't take kindly to my attitude and was suspicious of my behavior. I had two options, follow her to the police station to pay the fine or go to jail right now. All I could think about was getting out of town. Most of my paycheck went into that single transaction. After the police department released me, I got drunk that night with Jim at the bar. I said my goodbyes the next morning and drove alone to Karen's house in New Mexico.

I reached Karen's house about 2:00 a.m. the next morning, trembling and scared. She had been waiting up for me. She gave me a big hug and sent me to bed.

In the morning, I told Karen all the sordid details about what had happened in Oklahoma. It seemed to frighten her. She was afraid they would trace me to her house and problems would arise for her family. Karen called my mother in Clear Lake, California, and sent me off to see her.

I was hesitant. "I don't really want to live with my mom again," I told her.

"She's looking forward to seeing you," Karen coaxed. "She even promised to help you get an apartment and get you back on your feet. She loves you Kathy, she'll do the right thing for you."

Reluctantly I agreed. Karen gave me some pocket money for gas and food before sending me on my way. I never saw or heard from her again. She even disconnected herself from my mother, for which I was solely to blame.

Driving through Kingman Arizona, on my way back to California, the engine on the VW had problems again. I pulled into a service station and parked in the back. I slept there until morning, cold, alone, and frightened. Once again I called my father.

"Dad, what's your credit card number?"

"Kathy, is that you?" he said with a sleepy voice.

"Dad, I'm in Kingman, Arizona and there is a problem with the car again."

That wasn't an easy phone call to make. My father obliged me and provided his credit card once again, after expressing a few expletives. I stayed there all day as the engine was removed and some rubber seals were replaced. Then I hit the road. I had to stop during the middle of the night for sleep somewhere near Bakersfield. I had only thirty dollars left to my name, but I desperately needed a shower and a safe place to rest. I found a hotel that was still open and a clerk willing to take my cash in exchange for a dirty room. I wondered how many times it had been used that night as I pulled the covers up over my head to sleep.

When I reached Clear Lake I was nervous. It had been a long time since I had seen my mother, and I didn't know what to expect. I knocked on the door to a lovely home with a well-manicured yard facing the lake.

From inside I could hear my mother's voice say, "Cocoa, your sister is here."

When she opened the door there was a toy poodle in her arms.

"Kathy, meet Cocoa," she said cheerfully.

I thought, "Great! Is it not enough that I've been called a dog all my life – now I'm related to one too?"

She was kind and very welcoming. My mother's home was beautifully decorated and meticulously clean. After she showed me around she invited me to lunch. While we were visiting I asked her if she really planned to help me get an apartment.

"Yes," she replied.

"Could we look at some this afternoon so I can see what's available?"

She agreed. We drove around town and looked at several really nice places, some more expensive than I could afford. But I did settle on one I thought was within my earning ability.

"Mom," I said nervously, "I think I need to get a job before renting something."

"Okay," she said. "Suit yourself."

So I asked her to stop at a local restaurant so I could inquire about a position inside. They hired me as a waitress on the spot. I was so excited, thinking I finally could get back on my feet and start over.

When we returned to the house I could hear mom in conversation with Pappy in the other room. I didn't think much about it and assumed all would progress as planned. But when I asked if she would loan me the money for the least expensive apartment available, she turned me down.

"No, we think you ought to stay here for a few weeks. We are leaving for a trip in the motor home and you can house sit for us while we are gone. When we get back we can talk about the loan. I don't have the money now."

I felt betrayed and angry. "Well, that won't be necessary," I replied curtly, "I won't be staying."

"Where will you go? You don't have any money, do you?" she asked.

"I don't know where I'll go, but I don't belong here. Maybe you could just give me a tank of gas and I'll be on my way."

Pappy followed me to the gas station, put ten dollars in my tank, and said goodbye.

I was so hurt and angry, and screamed and cried as I drove toward San Jose.

It felt good to return to familiar territory, but I didn't know where to go once I arrived. I pulled the car up alongside John and Kimberly's house and slept in the front seat until morning.

From the time I ran away from home at fourteen, until I reached adulthood, I was a wandering vagabond with one foot in the street at every turn. By the age of eighteen I had lived in my car and moved thirty-two times in four years.

Chapter 7

Denial of the Obvious

In a desperate attempt to get out from under my family's watchful eye, I moved in with Sam, a man I hardly knew. I paid rent, cleaned the house, took care of his little boy and was available for any sexual interest. Clearly, Sam made out well with this deal. I wasn't very concerned about this arrangement until the evening Angelica entered our lives. She knocked on the door looking for Sam. She was beautiful with long blonde hair and big blue eyes, a native of Germany. She was smart, sexy, and carried herself with European sophistication. Sam was drawn to her like a moth to a flame.

As the odd man out, I started looking for alternate living arrangements and moved back in with my father while Jean was visiting her home in the Philippines. Angelica left Sam shortly after I did and I invited her to move in with my father and me for a short time. She wasted no time putting her assets to work for an escort service and made more money in one evening than I could make in a week. My father became suspicious of her activities and I knew we had to be out of his house before Jean returned to the states. We blended our funds to rent an apartment together.

My sister-in-law helped me find temporary clerical work with a military contractor in Silicon Valley, offering a better career path and income than retail health food stores. But every month I struggled to make ends meet. The temptation to join Angelica as a high class "lady of the evening" was considerable. There was just one problem; I was continually hemorrhaging. At Angelica's insistence, I finally went to a specialist to determine the problem.

When the doctor examined me he said, "When did you have the baby?"

"What baby?" I asked.

"Well there is scarring from a vaginal birth. I need to know how recent this was."

"I don't know what you are talking about," I replied.

I got dressed and then he sat me down in his office and very gently asked, "Kathy is your father sexually abusing you?"

"NO," I said emphatically.

He leaned back in his chair and thought for a moment. Then he ordered a D&C and several tests. My father insisted on coming to these appointments with me to talk to the doctor. I was very uncomfortable and nothing improved with the treatment. Looking back now, I consider the "problem" to have been a blessing that saved me from a life of prostitution.

At nineteen, I went to work as a configuration analyst. While there, I met Jack Price. He was a drafter in the engineering department and professed to be a Christian scholar and to hold a PhD in psychology. Jack loved to engage people in philosophic discussions about the pyramids in Egypt and to discuss controversy surrounding the Bible. What he lacked in looks, he made up for in personality. Jack became somewhat of a friend and mentor to me. Although I had no romantic interest in him, I did enjoy intellectual bantering and discussion with him. Jack clumsily tried to woo me into a romantic relationship and frequently invited me out for lunch or drinks after work.

Angelica moved to LA to become a model, and I rented my own place in downtown San Jose. I continued to have phone contact with my family but I delighted in my ability to support myself financially and finally live on my own.

In October 1983, I received a phone call from my father that changed my life.

"Kathy, we are having a family meeting tonight, you need to be here. Come over right away," he demanded.

"I can't Dad, I have plans," I replied. "Maybe I can come by after work tomorrow."

"It's important. I need to talk to you," he insisted.

"Well, can't you just tell me now?" I countered.

"No, it's not that simple," he said with an edge of frustration in his voice.

He didn't tell me what was wrong, but I knew before I put down the phone. He had cancer. I spoke with Jack about it.

"All those years I begged him to quit smoking and now he wants me to run over there so he can tell me he has cancer," I complained.

Jack replied, "You don't know that's what he wants to discuss with you."

"Yes I do. I just know it," I said angrily.

I drove to dad's house the next day after work and was given the news I expected. The cancer was pervasive and had spread from his lungs to the bones in his ribcage. It was inoperable. The doctor gave him two months to live.

It was difficult for me to focus at work, and periodically I had to run to the ladies room to sob. The grieving process was relentless. In mid-December, Jack and I took a Christmas tree to dad's house. Dad was in good spirits. He joined us in the living room to share old stories while we decorated the tree. Two weeks later he was in too much pain to get out of bed.

Pneumonia hit him next, and we thought for sure we would lose him. Jean and I kept vigil all night while dad was in the hospital. He cried out for his mother during the night, then went back to sleep. Somehow he survived pneumonia and the surgery to remove the cancer from his neck. Then it reached his brain and we put him in a hospice center.

Angelica came to visit from LA to comfort me. She said, "Where I come from we do things differently. We don't let people suffer like that. Why don't you just take a shotgun in there and put him out of his misery?" she said matter-of-factly.

I screamed, "Don't say that. You have no right to say that. Get out!"

She promptly left and I curled up in a ball on the bathroom floor and wailed for hours.

During the months of dad's illness, Jack spent a significant amount of time with both my father and me, attempting to support and comfort us both. Twice he proposed to marry me, but I declined.

On March 20, 1984, the hospice nurse called about 7:30 a.m. Dad had passed away. Two days later, Jack proposed again, and this time I accepted.

Chapter 8

The Ribbon Unravels

I continued therapy with Joanna for nearly eight months before our first breakthrough came.

After listening to me complain about financial problems and the boys for the umpteenth time she said, "Kathy you don't trust God, do you?"

"No," I replied. "Why should I? He's not there for me. The last time I trusted God He took everything from me."

"I see," said Joanna, with a knowing, wry little smile. "How about we test that assumption?"

"What do you mean?" I asked.

"Well," she began, "I want you to make a list of all of the things you are worried about every day. List everything from grocery money, to problems with the kids. Then, I want you to pray over the list. Ask God to meet your needs and then give the list to Him. Put the list in a box or a can labeled "God can" and don't look at it for a week. At the end of that time, read your list and check off every item that God took care of for you that week."

I thought it was corny, but I was willing to give it a try. To my surprise, within the first week over half of the items on the list had been resolved. It was the first tangible evidence I had that God was working on my behalf since I was saved, almost five years earlier.

Aware that my distrust in God seemed to stem from my

relationship with Jack, Joanna said gently, "Why don't you tell me about your first marriage?"

I agreed to marry Jack just days after my father died, in March 1984. I figured it was not only time to settle down, but I also felt a lot of pressure from the family to marry this man so they wouldn't have to worry about me. Jean was pushing the hardest. She seemed to have a relationship with Jack I wasn't privy to. Shortly after my father's death, I overheard Jack and Jean talking privately about my father and guns in the Philippines. It struck me as odd, but I filed it somewhere in the back of my mind without saying anything.

After Jean returned to the Philippines with dad's ashes, Jack and I planned our wedding. It gave me something to look forward to and it seemed to repress the grief. I went to work making my wedding dress and putting all of the details together for the special day. While I sat on the bed watching TV and cutting fabric, the Easter Story about Jesus played on the screen. I had heard of Jesus at the Baptist church when I was a kid, but I didn't know anything about Him. I watched with curiosity, and something warm and peaceful stirred in my spirit. Thereafter I had cold feet about the wedding. But every time I felt like backing out, Jack came on strong.

We made plans for a July wedding and a reception at Zorba, a Greek family restaurant. Why we chose that place I have no idea, but they did have a beautiful rose garden and patio area in the back for the ceremony. I wanted to give Jack an extravagant gift, so I took out a loan to buy him a solid oak piano and had it delivered the night before the wedding. Angelica made us a beautiful wedding cake and sang "Evergreen" for us on the piano. Everyone I knew was there: my mother and Pappy, John, Jerry, Tanya, and all of their spouses and children. Monique was my maid of honor in a lovely peach-colored maternity dress.

As I stood poised and ready to walk down the aisle, Monique

leaned over and said, "Kathy you don't have to do this. Don't you realize you are marrying your father?"

I shuddered, but at that point it was too late – the guests had arrived and the music was playing. I couldn't back out. Nor did I realize the full ramifications of what I was about to do.

Jack was more than twice my age. I loved him, but I wasn't "in-love" with him. Monique was right. Jack was every bit my father. He wore my father's tailored suits, could wear his shoes, and even wore the same ring size. They shared the same receding hairline and rotting teeth. A year after we were married, Jack and I moved east to start a new life and raise a family in Connecticut.

The Norman Rockwell family of my imagination was beginning to take shape in my mind. We would live in the country, have several children, and live happily ever after.

We arrived in Connecticut with a station wagon loaded to the top and two dogs we had adopted. John promptly found a job and we rented a lovely little white house on Dooley's pond. It was a dream come true for me. During the day I cleaned and prepared our new home. At night we went to the local pub for entertainment. Jack and I enjoyed drinking brandy and listening to jazz.

Kitty Katherine was singing one night. She had a beautiful voice and the charm and charisma of a Broadway star. During her break, Kitty joined us at the table and struck-up a lively conversation. She asked us where we were from and which church we went to. We told her we were new to the area and would like to find a nice church. The next Sunday we met Kitty at a little white country church designed for a picture postcard. Kitty got up to sing and belted out the most beautiful gospel songs I had ever heard. Before I left church that day, I accepted Jesus as my Lord and Savior. The concept of Christianity seemed "safe," a "good idea," or "the right thing to do." It was an intellectual decision I made at the time with my head and not my heart. The Norman Rockwell family went to church right?

The next time I sat in church my mind wandered. I struggled to read the Bible and I was distracted in church. I remember staring at the pastor from the front pew, imagining him naked. I wondered what was wrong with me that such a wicked thought would cross my mind.

The pastor and his wife warmly welcomed us into their home, as did Kitty and her family. We were building a life with friends and a new family in a quaint little community. We often spent the night at Kitty's and I grew to really love her.

I recall vividly the day she looked me in the eyes and told me "You'll know you are really saved when you quit smoking."

I didn't really understand. Was I saved or not saved? I had no intention of quitting smoking at twenty. The pastor told me it was important that I get baptized. I saw it as a way to really "seal the deal." So I did. Soon after, however, very strange things began to happen.

It was late autumn and I noticed a swarm of flies pummeling our bedroom window, from the inside! Sometime later, from that same window, I noticed a long string of moving candlelight behind the pond. I was later told there were witches worshiping in the woods behind our house. Another evening when we visited the pastor and his wife, we were startled by strange sounds that came up from the basement of the parsonage. The best way I could describe the sound was rolling granite. New to the faith, I did not understand the spiritual battle warring all around me. I was frightened and perplexed. Jack seemed nervous.

Coming home from work one day Jack announced that he had quit his job. Unable to pay the rent, we knew we would have to move out. I recall writing a bad check at the grocery store for food. That same evening the church took up a special offering for us – in the exact amount of the bad check. It felt like proof to me that God was real and He cared about our situation.

We put our dogs in a kennel and our furniture in storage until John found temporary work in Norwalk and then we moved into a trashy motel. After three months on that job he quit again. This time no employer would have him. Desperate, we took our dogs from the kennel to the pound, sold our furniture, and packed our station wagon for a return trip to California.

My mother said she would take us in. We stayed with her for three weeks, until I overheard her screaming to Pappy about how lazy and awful we were, and how she didn't want to support us. I felt betrayed again. She didn't seem to understand that job hunting is like farming. It takes some time for resumes to harvest.

We left LA that night for San Jose with a bag of peanut butter sandwiches and ten bucks for gas. With nowhere else to go I contacted my friend Matthew and his wife Sally. They took us in, fed us, counseled us, and even paid our bills. We weren't there long before we lost the engine on the station wagon. All that remained of my life with Jack at that point was our marriage.

During our stay with Matthew and Sally, they became suspicious of Jack. After helping us file our taxes for the year, they ran Jack's social security number through an emergency room computer that Sally had access to as a nurse. Matthew and Sally started fighting frequently. I asked them what was going on. They looked at each other, and invited me to lunch with them at Denny's. Upon my insistence they finally shared their findings with me.

They said, "Jack has a 'rap' sheet three feet long."

He was wanted in New York for alimony and back child support for an ex-wife and two children I didn't know about. He owed back taxes and there was a warrant out for his arrest for assaulting a police officer.

The wheels turned in my head as the picture became clear. Jack had even lied on our marriage license. Our life in Connecticut was likely a sham to provide proximity for him to visit his children. His three-month job-hopping was done to avoid the attachment of his wages for back child support in New York state. I was devastated.

Matthew loaned me the money to rent an apartment and I was hired for a temporary job the next day. He threw what remained of my belongings in his car and bought me a card table, fold-up chairs, and an air mattress to furnish the apartment and help me get started. Matthew had been my boss when I worked for a little entrepreneurial company at seventeen. Somehow we always stayed in touch. But I wondered why he was so generous with me. Then he hugged me and confessed his long time affection and interest in me, implying I owed him something more than money. I didn't know what to do but tell him it wasn't good timing and thank him for all he had done for me. There was no way I could ever repay him.

The apartment was walking distance from my new job at Westinghouse. I settled in quickly and then recognized an old boss from a previous temporary position.

He pulled me aside on my first day and whispered, "Whatever you do, do not bring your personal problems to work. Agreed?"

"Okay," I replied as stoically as possible. Little did he know my life had just fallen apart and it was all I could do to stand up straight.

When I came home from work, Jack was waiting for me at the apartment.

"What are you doing here?" I said curtly.

He said, "I just wanted to see you and talk to you for a few minutes."

Like an idiot I let him in. He sat on the couch and we made light conversation. Then he looked at me with big puppy eyes and said, "I want you back. If you were really a Christian you would forgive me."

I lost my temper at that point and yelled, "I forgive you, now get the hell out of my house and don't ever come back."

Later Matthew told me Jack walked ten miles to Milpitas for a place to sleep that night. Matthew and Sally supported him a few more weeks until he found a job and moved to LA where we had originally distributed resumes. Shortly thereafter, I received a phone call from his nutty new girlfriend in LA. After a few minutes of speaking with her I knew he never loved me, he was already shacking up with someone else.

Although I was making a reasonable wage in the new job, the discouraging fact was that at the end of every week, after the bills were paid, I had just fourteen dollars left to buy food. The combined total of marriage debt was well over forty thousand dollars, most of which was in my name at Jack's insistence. I knew I couldn't afford an attorney so I began looking for creative solutions. I tried to sell my wedding gown at a consignment shop but there were no takers. Desperate, I sold my wedding bands with the intention of using the money to pay a paralegal to file for an annulment. Instead, I drank the money at a local bar with a friend that night. I went to see the paralegal anyway.

She said, "Honey you need to do two things. First, you need to go out and buy yourself a fine new car. Put a few miles on it and stop paying your bills. You need to file for both a bankruptcy and an annulment. For a hundred and fifty dollars I will show you how to rebuild your credit with the car and you will be able to start over. I'll walk you through all of the paperwork and you'll be just fine."

At twenty-two, I represented myself in court for both petitions and both proceedings were finalized in my favor.

I was lonely and living on the edge with high anxiety. It was probably the closest I could have been to a nervous breakdown, although things continued to get worse.

I went to visit Monique hoping for the comfort of an old friend, but all she said was, "I told you so. Don't come crying to me."

Very hurt, and feeling completely betrayed, I cried all the way back to my apartment.

At that point I turned my back on God. I sought comfort in promiscuous sexual relationships. Living on alcohol, cigarettes, and coffee, I lost weight like an anchor. Anorexia had kicked in again and I was literally wasting my life away. When I was alone at night, thoughts of suicide plagued me and I often drank myself to sleep. I was scolded more than once because the smell of alcohol was still on my breath when I reported for work in the morning.

The pastor and his wife called from Connecticut to find out how we were doing. After filling them in on all the news I said, "If this is Christianity, I don't want anything to do with it. I've lost everything: the station wagon died as soon as we got here. All of the furniture is gone, I gave up my dogs, the marriage is over, and so are my dreams for the future. If this is how my life is with God, I'll do just fine without him."

There was a long pause on the other end of the line and Nora, the pastor's wife, said, "This is the best time to reach out to God. Find a new church and start over Kathy."

I thanked them for calling but never spoke with them again.

Reviewing my circumstances I had to ask myself some hard questions. "How could I have been married to a man for two years and not recognize his deception? How could I be so gullible, so incredibly stupid? How is it that everyone else could see it but me?" It finally dawned on me that I needed help. I pulled the name of a counselor out of the phone book and started weekly sessions. That was the beginning of my recovery.

The cost of therapy was another financial challenge as soon as my new car payments were due. Macy's hired me as a sales clerk to work evening and weekend shifts. I did my best to manage the stress of both jobs. But there were subtle signs I was losing ground. During the White Flower Day sale on Saturday, I sent a customer home with an empty watch box. I pressed forward until I just couldn't manage it all anymore.

When I quit, the HR representative said, "Well, some people can handle two jobs. Obviously you are not one of them."

Joanna seemed to understand where my faith was crushed, but exhorted me to face those feelings and try again. Today I realize God stripped my life of everything that was not of Him, and began a long and arduous rebuilding process. The Master Creator began by wiping away my old life so He could give me a new life starting from scratch. Although I walked away from Him, He never left me. Instead He waited until I came back to Him and gave Him my heart.

Chapter 9

New Beginnings

My old drinking buddy Robert came over to the apartment after I had gotten settled. It had been about four years since I had seen him. He looked terrific as always. We poured some wine and he joined me at my makeshift table.

He said, "Kathy, there's something I have to tell you."

"Yeah," I said blowing cigarette smoke in his face playfully.

"You've been gone awhile and I've changed." His tone was really serious, calling for my attention. Then he finally spit out the words, "I'm gay."

"Really?" I replied with a squeal.

We talked for hours, finished the bottle of cheap wine, and filled an ashtray. Robert and I were good friends, somehow always able to pick up where we left off. He needed a place to stay, and I needed a friend. Robert moved in with me the next day. During the months that followed we partied much like we had done years before. When I would leave for the evening he would teasingly ask if I remembered my "whore bag," a vinyl pouch filled with toiletries. I'm ashamed to even recall my behavior at that time.

After Halloween, despair hit me and I felt suicidal again. I didn't know what was wrong with me, but I was in deep emotional anguish. Robert stood by me and tried to talk me through it and I continued to see my counselor. After several months the counselor confronted me with the fact that I was using men as a drug, in the same way an addict reaches for cocaine. I decided to cut myself off cold turkey. Severe depression took hold and I felt terribly lonely, even in a room full of people. The deepest need in my heart was intimacy, but I had none of lasting value.

On a crisp, cool Saturday morning in February, I decided to go to the park where my father took me once or twice when I was a child. I just needed to hear the sound of children laughing and playing. I took along a blanket and some books, and settled myself on a little bluff overlooking the playground at Vasona Park. I was writing a letter to Angelica as a soft breeze blew through the trees. A man walked by and made a comment about the psychology paperback lying on my blanket. He wore gray velour drawstring pants and a matching sweatshirt.

"Hi, I'm Carl," he said as he plopped himself down on my blanket.

I remember thinking, "Wow, if there was ever a need for an expiration date on clothing, here it is." He was warm and friendly with a receding hairline and gorgeous blue eyes. We started talking and didn't stop for nearly three hours. His boys Lee, eight years old at the time, and Eddy, ten, came by to check in periodically as we chatted. Carl claimed to be a karate expert and a long-distance runner. This intrigued me, so I challenged him to a race around the Foothill College par course. He agreed to meet me there.

I was driving my brand new Mazda with red racing stripes and he was driving an old Dodge Aspen. When he met me at the college, he let the boys out of the car to play, and promptly changed into running shorts behind the open door. I was a little surprised, thinking "this guy's got chutzpah."

The course was a few miles long, over rolling hills and

through breathtaking scenery, in the Los Altos foothills. Carl later told me he was just following the smell of my perfume, but I beat him fair and square. After the run we stopped at a little market where I had a beer and a smoke.

"You smoke?" he asked, incredulous.

"Yeah, I know I need to quit."

"I'm just surprised," he replied. "How can you be in such good shape and smoke?"

"I don't know," I said. But of course, I was only twenty-two years old.

Carl was a good twelve years my senior. We left in separate cars and agreed to meet again sometime. I gave him my number, but he didn't call. A week later I called him and asked if he would like a running partner.

I said, "I just want to be friends, nothing more than that. I really enjoy your company."

We decided to meet again for a run, then later a movie. Then came the day when I had to explain living with Robert. That made for an uncomfortable conversation.

Robert asked me how things were going with Carl.

I said, "Great! He might even be the 'one,' you know?" To which he replied, "Be careful what you ask for, you might just get it."

I quit smoking and started taking better care of myself, running almost every day. Soon thereafter, Robert moved out and Carl and the boys moved in. This arrangement was just for a short while until we could rent a place of our own, large enough for all of us. I loved the boys and wanted to mother them. Unfortunately, the mothering modeled to me was that of the authoritarian parent, which promptly pushed them away. If there was one regret in my life, that would be it. I wish I had approached them more as a friend than a drill sergeant.

Carl had a good stable job, and I secured a good position at

Lockheed. We were both doing well and prospering financially. We rented a nice little three-bedroom home in Cupertino and played house. We fought from time to time and the relationship became quite stormy. I think we both questioned remaining in the relationship.

After complaining of flu symptoms that lasted for days, I finally went to the doctor.

He said, "Well, I'm an old country doctor, but if you ask me, I'd say you're pregnant."

"What?" I exclaimed out loud.

The thought had not occurred to me. In all the years of running around I had never gotten pregnant and wondered if I ever could. For the two years I was married to Jack, I begged God to give me a baby. In His mercy He didn't. But this was different. I was speechless.

Carl and I decided to meet for lunch at the park in Sunnyvale. I told him I was prepared to take care of the baby on my own.

"No," he said. "This is *our* baby. Let's see if we can make this relationship work."

We married in October 1988, beneath the big oak tree in the backyard of my brother John's house in Morgan Hill. I couldn't find a wedding gown to hide five months, so I made my dress again. In the interest of time, I stitched Velcro in place of buttons. I also made the cake, but when the time came to frost it, three of its layers broke and landed in the sink. My matron of honor ran to the local grocery store for a cake while I sobbed in the bathroom.

It was a lovely California day. When it was time, we all assembled in our places and my brother John started the CD with the wedding march. My little niece waited at the patio door prepared to lead the procession. When she heard the music she ran out with the flowers, and realizing she was too far ahead of us, she ran back inside the house crying. No amount of coaxing could bring her back out. As the video camera captured the action, my mother tried to hide behind a patio post. Unfortunately, she stuck out rather like a raspberry barrel on all sides in her knit dress. The wind blew; it blew all of the plastic cups off the table. The pastor was a woman who sounded too much like Elmer Fudd.

"Do you pwomise to wuv honow and chawish…"

Then as we were saying our vows, the rooster in the backyard started doodling, an airplane soared overhead, and the guests started laughing hysterically. Carl and I looked like two deer caught in headlights.

When my mother saw the video she laughed so hard I thought she was going to wet her pants.

"I'm sorry honey," she said wiping her eyes, "I know this was important to you, but I just can't stop laughing."

We teased about sending the video to America's Funniest Home Videos for years, but never did it.

After the wedding it seemed Christmas came right away. Then we started Lamaze classes and our little family prepared for the blessed birth of our baby. My relationship with Carl improved dramatically with the marriage commitment and the boys began to settle into our new life together. In January, I was about seven months along when the joy of pregnancy turned into panic attacks and night terrors. Insomnia struck me hard, like a hammer from the past. Every night when I laid down to sleep, fear and trauma assailed me.

The doctor said, "Once you have the baby you'll be fine Kathy."

I tried acupuncture and called the counselor I had seen a couple of years earlier, yet could not explain or stop the night terrors.

Marie was born full-term, by cesarean after thirty-six hours of labor. It was as though my body would not release her and refused to dilate. I was awake during the surgery, but I almost lost it when the nurses left the room with my baby.

"Carl," I screamed, "Stay with the baby."

He did. He followed the nurses as they cleaned her and suctioned the gunk from her lungs. When they finally put her in my arms I just wept with joy. We both did. She was so beautiful. They say babies can't smile when they are first born, but Marie did. She looked right at the top of Carl's balding forehead and smiled. I counted all of her little fingers and toes. She was perfect. That night after Carl and the boys went home to sleep I nursed my baby girl and spoke softly to her for hours making parenting promises that I couldn't keep.

Well after Marie's birth I still had trouble sleeping. At night I was always listening for sounds in the house and walking through the rooms vigilant, as though expecting an intruder. I couldn't really rest unless my baby was sleeping on my chest and I could feel her breathing. I was terribly overprotective and wouldn't even let the boys play with her.

Lockheed called and asked me when I was coming back to work. I said, "I'll have to get back to you."

When Carl got home that night I got on my knees crying and I said, "I'll do anything, scrub toilets, wipe butts – anything to stay home with my baby. I can't go back to work and leave her with a stranger," I sobbed.

That night my daycare was born.

The new baby got all of the attention in the house from both Carl and me. Eddy and Lee were left to their own resources, feeling terribly rejected and abandoned by their father. It wasn't long before they both started having trouble in school and the school counselor recommended counseling for Carl and me. That's how we met Joanna, when Marie was only two months old.

Chapter 10

Breakthrough

On October 17 1989, the last of our daycare kids left the house with their parents at 5:00 p.m. I was feeding Marie creamed carrots in the infant swing, when suddenly the entire house began to shake. The glass on the patio doors behind the baby moved like liquid, the microwave was bouncing on the counter. Finally, it registered – earthquake! Afraid the glass on the full-length window behind Marie would shatter, I yanked her out of the baby swing. The contents of the kitchen cabinets poured onto the kitchen floor, crashing and breaking in a tumultuous clatter.

I could hardly hold my footing as I screamed for Eddy and Lee – "EARTHQUAKE!"

By some miracle Carl and both boys were home. We huddled in the hallway safe from falling objects, listening to things crashing in the rooms all around us. Lee suddenly bolted for the front door with Eddy right behind him.

"Stop," I screamed. "Don't go outside!"

Just then the thirty-gallon fish tank in the living room crashed to the ground. Fish were flopping in the gravel and water flooded the carpet. Marie was crying. I had bruised her little legs while pulling her from the baby swing to safety. Carl stayed calm and called the boys. We huddled in the hallway until it was all over. Those moments seemed so long while we waited for the shaking to stop.

Together, we peeked out the front door. One by one doors opened up and down the street as neighbors peered outside. Water from the pool across the street was lapping at the grass in our front yard. For a moment there was an eerie silence. No one dared say a word. Then, as though a sound switch had been flipped, sirens went off all over the area. Our neighbor met me on the lawn, we were both weeping.

"Is this it? Is this Armageddon?" I wondered.

Carl went through the house to survey the damage. Pictures had fallen from the walls; plants had toppled to the floor. The desk had shimmied two feet from the wall and a bottle of salad dressing broke and mixed in with the shattered dishes on the floor. The electricity was out and it was getting dark. We couldn't put the baby down anywhere due to the glass and debris on the floor. Carl erected a tent outside for all of us and moved sleeping bags and the playpen out there for Marie. I sometimes teased Carl and called him MacGyver because he could make a tool out of anything as long as there was duct tape handy. He got the boys busy making camp and fired up the barbecue to grill hot dogs for dinner.

News reports announced the quake was a 7.2. Aftershocks hit periodically for two weeks following the big quake, keeping me in a constant state of vigilance. The electricity was out for three days, so we roughed it camping in the backyard. In the meantime we moved all of the living room furniture onto the lawn and pulled up all of the water-soaked carpeting in the front half of the house. Two blocks up the street we could hear the sound of glass shattering in the big dumpsters behind the grocery store. Carl fashioned cupboard stops to hold the cabinets closed during aftershocks and the landlord ordered a house inspection and new carpeting. The worst structural damage was a crack in the fireplace, rendering it useless. The rest was a matter of cleanup.

The earthquake did more than scare me; it made me realize it was time to get right with God. It was reported that churches were overflowing all across Silicon Valley that month. For the first time in almost four years, I went back to church. I found a little Bible church nearby.

During my first visit, I went up to the altar, got on my knees, and asked God to forgive me for walking away. I surrendered my heart to Him. It was a commitment I didn't make the first time, but knew I had to make now. The pastor and his wife prayed for me that morning and I came home from church absolutely elated. I couldn't explain it, but God had touched my heart. I had no idea what He had prepared for the years ahead, but renewing my relationship with Him was the most critical part of my recovery.

I saw Joanna on a weekly basis for eight months before my first breakthrough. Each session I valiantly swung at the leaves on the tree of my heart, expressing minor complaints and avoiding the deep issues that could only be found at the roots. I knew I needed more courage than I could muster to face the truth inside me. I danced around that tree until I could do it no more. By April the following year, I was four months pregnant again, and increasingly uncomfortable with burgeoning feelings I tried to suppress.

Joanna said, "It takes a lot of energy to hold a beach ball down in the water. That's what it is like for you as you try to suppress what you are feeling. The insomnia is just a symptom Kathy. It's a symptom of something deeper."

Then Joanna pulled out a drawing pad and crayons and asked me if I would like to draw what it felt like when I couldn't sleep. I recoiled at the thought as if I had touched a hot stove. Then I insisted it was time for me to leave.

"I'll see you next week then?" She asked.

I nodded and scrambled for the door.

The next time I visited Joanna she suggested we try something else.

"It's called eye-movement desensitization and reprocessing or EMDR."

She described it as a way to relax the brain similar to the way reading works at bedtime when you move your eyes left to right. The technique worked in such a way that would allow a subconscious memory to surface, but I would still be in control. I agreed to try it. Joanna asked me to focus on her hand as she slowly moved it back and forth before my eyes. Then I closed my eyes and saw a vivid picture of my childhood bedroom. The bed was against the wall, opposite the closet, and toys were scattered on the floor. I was wearing a red nightgown.

As I described the image to Joanna, I told her I thought I was about three years old. My father was in the room. He was naked. He held me to the floor and lifted my nightgown. The memory retrieval lasted just moments then it stopped. I was shocked. I didn't know what to say. It was like a movie about someone else.

"How do you feel?" Joanna asked gently.

"I don't know," I said pausing. "I feel numb. I don't have any feelings."

Joanna was surprised at my response. "Usually incest memories are gut-wrenching," she said.

"Oh," I replied.

She studied my face carefully and said, "Either there is a tremendous amount of disassociation going on, or this is just the tip of the iceberg."

I gave her a flat expression. "Maybe this information just needs to soak in," I replied.

Instead of going home after the session, I drove up to the top of a nearby hill and parked where I could see the city lights stretch for miles. I just sat there running the images over and over in my mind telling myself, "my father sexually abused me, and I was just a little girl…" The denial was thick. I didn't want to believe it, but deep down I knew it was true. I also knew there was more to remember. In the days that followed I felt a sense of relief, no longer holding down the beach ball, I could relax, the secret was finally out.

I told Carl what I remembered and he was very sympathetic.

"We kind of figured something happened, didn't we? The way you had your dad up on that pedestal I knew someday he would come crashing down," Carl said.

"Yeah, this just changes everything I ever thought about my dad. It's going to take me a while to get my head wrapped around it," I replied.

Shortly thereafter I came into Marie's room where Carl was getting her ready for bed. He started to pull a red nightgown over her head when I shouted.

"Oh no! Put something else on her."

"Kathy, what's the matter?" Carl asked confused.

"I just… I was wearing a red nightgown when my father abused me," I sobbed.

Carl reached out his hand to me, "It's alright," he said. "No one is going to hurt our little girl."

"Take that nightgown off of her, now. I just can't stand to see her in it."

Patiently, he pulled off the red nightgown and put our little girl in pajamas.

I exclaimed, "How can I protect her? How can I trust any man around my beautiful baby girl?"

Carl reassured me over and over again. He promised he would never touch her. I wanted to believe him, but words were not enough.

Subsequent sessions with Joanna produced additional memories. Sometimes I just remembered one "sense" of the experience like a picture or an emotion. Other times I felt the physical body sensations of being molested but couldn't see any pictures and didn't know the identity of my perpetrator. Probably the most difficult part of the experience was the leaking emotions that came unexpectedly and were disconnected from current activities. Feelings of anger, fear, and betrayal swept through me like a firestorm. Joanna explained how emotions are repressed in the mind and need to be expressed for the healing to occur. She said the fact that I was remembering things in such small fragments indicated a higher degree of traumatic intensity because my mind separated the reality into individual senses to cope with the information.

One night, as I was beginning to slip off to sleep, I could smell my father in the room. It was a sickening mixture of Old Spice and cigarettes. As I lay there I could feel him having sex with me. I didn't know whether I was dreaming or awake. Fear jolted me conscious and I shook Carl. "Honey, wake up."

"What's the matter?" he said groggy.

"It's my dad. I don't know whether it's his spirit, or a memory, or a dream or what," I cried. "I could feel him on me." I shuddered and said, "I just feel so dirty. What's wrong with me?" I sobbed. "Just hold me, please," I begged.

Carl comforted me as best he could, and then he went back to sleep. But I lay there awake for hours tossing back and forth and making trips to the bathroom.

Joanna urged me to continue pressing forward into the feelings with each new picture that floated up. Each week seemed to bring with it a new memory, more emotionally intense and physically traumatic. Soon we realized I needed more support than a weekly counseling session could offer. Joanna suggested a support group for incest survivors that I began to attend regularly. It wasn't easy to sit in a room full of people and talk about what I was going through, but it was helpful to know I wasn't the only one. I joined a group that met every Sunday evening, and before long I looked forward to being there. One particular meeting remains etched in my memory.

I said, "Hi, my name is Kathy and I am an incest survivor."

The group welcomed me and smiled, listening quietly. I took a deep breath and began to share what had happened that week to me.

"I woke up with really sore hands. Both my hands and my forearms were all red. It was the strangest thing. Later that day the pictures came up to explain it." I started weeping, but the room remained silent while I continued to share.

I could see pictures of our backyard when I was about five years old. It must have been a Saturday because my dad was home but my mom was nowhere around. My neighbor friend Rachel was over and we were playing in the backyard together. The next thing I remembered my dad was on top of me on the cement and I was slapping the hard concrete with my hands and forearms trying to get free. Then he went after Rachel. I couldn't stop him. I felt so responsible for my friend. Everything inside me would have preferred him to hurt me rather than her. I just couldn't stop him, I couldn't protect her…

Tears fell like raindrops. When I finished, another survivor spoke up and shared her story. It was a safe place to be real for a time, but afterwards I had to face life at home.

It felt like I was living in two worlds at the same time, the past and the present. Everything was happening so fast and my world was turning upside down. I reached a point where I wanted to stop, and get off the ride.

Joanna said, "Kathy, I wish I could tell you this would be easy, but it's not. As a matter of fact it will likely get worse before it gets better."

"I don't know if I can take it," I said softly. "Every day is different. One minute I'm fine, the next minute I'm raging or crying or something. I can't stop thinking about the abuse. I just want it to stop. I don't want to remember anything else."

"Kathy, do you remember telling me you want more than anything in the world to keep your children safe?"

"Yeah."

Joanna continued, "The most important thing you can do to protect your children is to deal with your stuff. It's the secrets in the mind, those hidden traumas that will seek to replay themselves in your life and theirs if not dealt with. If you don't want to recover for yourself, at least do it for your children. Talk about incest at home. It is the best way to prevent it. Your kids need you to be the best mom you can be," she said.

That struck a chord in me. I remembered my promises to Marie her first night in the world and decided to persevere.

"Okay," I said, wiping my eyes.

Joanna sighed, "I know this is tough, Kathy. From what I understand, it gets better after the first five years of therapy, but it is a very long road to recovery."

"Five years!" I exclaimed. "I don't think I can even handle one more year like this!"

"You will Kathy. One day at a time, you will get better," Joanna replied softly.

There were times when I could feel a memory surfacing and would consciously hold it back until the next time I would see Joanna. The memories were now surfacing so quickly that it became necessary for me to see her twice a week.

At one point God pulled back the thick blanket of amnesia and I remembered my earliest months in the world as though it was happening all over again. I recalled a particularly clear picture of my crib to the right of the window. I had been there crying for a long time. My face was wet and hot when my mother came in the room and slapped me, hard. I could hear her words.

"Stop it. **** it!" she yelled. "I can't stand it anymore, just stop it." She hit me again and left the room as swiftly as she entered.

I learned that my needs brought pain. I felt as though I wasn't worth feeding, and that I was going to starve because I was not lovable. I cried and cried, even screamed some more. No one came. Without words, every feeling was raw. Fear compounded upon fear within me. Had I been abandoned? Would I die? Who would take care of me?

My father brought a different kind of pain; a suffocating choking feeling that left me feeling hopeless and used. In one of my infant memories I was on the changing table. I could see him looming over me, and I didn't have words. I was abused. Joanna reached for me as I sputtered and coughed on her couch. I couldn't speak.

"Oh, I should have known this was coming. Kathy I'm so sorry. It's over now," Joanna said gently.

For days after that I wanted a soft blanket and bananas with Cream of Wheat cereal. I felt so small and full of emotion, without understanding. At times I just wanted to curl up in a little ball and suck my thumb. As I pulled out of that, the anger rose within me.

"He was a **** pedophile. How could he do that to an infant?" I raged.

That certainly wasn't all. Memories of other events, which occurred later, surfaced. I remembered a particular incident that happened before my father left for the Philippines when I was eight years old. He called me into his bedroom and had sex with me before I left for school. My mother was asleep down the hall. But somehow I cleaned myself up and went off to school as though it was just another day.

Joanna explained this as an example of the value of dissociation. One part of my mind took the abuse and hid it inside immediately, while in the other part I went to school and passed a spelling test as though nothing had happened. I could see the importance of being able to dissociate to survive.

Each memory felt like it removed structural beams from the foundation of my soul leaving only bitter truth where once lay denial.

By the end of July 1990, I was almost seven months pregnant with our son Bradley and battling severe insomnia again. Something dark from deep inside me was pressing on my conscious mind. I didn't know what it was. I couldn't explain the terror I felt. I was going through the same tormenting nights that I went through with Marie, at precisely the same point in the pregnancy. I was terrified, but I didn't know what it was. I would lay down to rest and my heart would pound. Slowly, at first, then faster and faster, gaining momentum until the anxiety rose in me like a tidal wave that crashed through my chest. I couldn't breathe. I couldn't speak. I just tossed and turned in the undulating current, drowning in fear, and at times even wetting the bed.

Sometimes I would get up and pace the floor so I wouldn't disturb Carl. One night in my wanderings, I was standing in the kitchen when I saw a black hooded figure flash before my eyes, and then disappear. I could feel the adrenaline rush in my veins. "What was that?" I thought. "Am I hallucinating?" I continued to pace the floor. I drank some milk. Then I prayed beseeching God's help. "Oh God what is happening to me? Am I losing my mind? Please help me."

I don't remember how or when I fell asleep that night. But shortly thereafter, I remember dreaming about my half-sister. In the dream she came to the door in the middle of the night with a bowl of blood. She was wearing a strange necklace with a five-pointed star inside a circle. I later discovered the necklace was a pentagram.

My mother called about this time. She asked me to fly out to Arizona to visit.

"I'll pay for your flight," she said sweetly.

"Oh I don't know mom, I'm so far along with this pregnancy and I have a daycare and Carl, Marie, and the boys to think about."

"Well, I'll pay to bring you all out here," she coaxed.

I felt suspicious; this degree of charity was uncharacteristic of her.

"I'll talk to Carl and my doctor about it and let you know," I replied.

My OB/GYN firmly said, "No, it isn't a good idea for you to fly so close to term."

I called my mom back and told her we'd come visit another time. She sounded disappointed. What I didn't know then, is clear today; that decision probably saved my baby's life.

Joanna and I had decided to postpone processing memories until after the baby was born to prevent any undue trauma to my unborn child. It seemed a reasonable decision. Joanna had planned a summer vacation and so we scheduled our next appointment two or three weeks after. I wanted to believe I could control the recovery process. With sheer willpower I was going to have memories when convenient in the schedule and when it made the most logical sense for my baby.

When Joanna returned from vacation, I described the dream to her. I also told her my mother had invited me to Phoenix for a visit. Joanna urged me to be cautious.

On August 3 1990, I felt terribly agitated and nervous. I was sleep-deprived and emotional all day. I felt a sense of intensity that I couldn't restrain.

Finally, I called Joanna and told her "I can feel a really bad memory coming. It feels so black and dark inside. This memory won't wait until after the baby is born. I can't hold it back, and I can't face it alone."

Joanna agreed to see me that afternoon.

I was scared. So scared I was almost nauseous. I didn't want to face this memory, but I knew if I waited it was going to burn through my consciousness on its own. I settled myself on Joanna's couch with my hands on my big pregnant belly. I took a big deep breath and told her I was ready. The room was electrically charged. The look on her face was pensive and serious.

"Okay, focus on the feeling and follow my fingers," she said, once again utilizing the eye-movement desensitization technique.

Immediately moving pictures of my childhood bedroom filled my mind. It was dark except for a string of candles placed on the dresser and along the windowsill. The people were dressed in black capes with hoods just like the image I had seen during the night. I could hear them chanting. At first I couldn't see their faces. Then I recognized my sister and her husband. They were passing a big silver challis filled with blood between them, and each drinking from it. The pictures stopped for a moment, my heart was pounding.

"Should we continue?" Joanna asked.

"Yes," I replied.

Joanna moved her hand before my eyes once again and I blinked.

"What do you see?" she asked.

"I can see myself. I'm naked and tied to a board with my legs spread. There are plastic sheets all over the floor."

Then a blood-curdling scream rose from the depths of my soul and shattered my consciousness like glass. "They are raping me, one after the other," I screamed.

Joanna jumped and held her breath. She was visibly shaken.

Resolutely I declared, "I can't do this," grabbing my purse

as I tried to pry myself up from the couch. I headed for the door sobbing.

"Wait," Joanna called after me. "Kathy," Joanna said. "We still have time."

"No, I can't. I can't do this anymore, I have to go home," I said.

I waddled out to the parking lot and climbed into the car, squeezing my pregnant belly behind the steering wheel. How I drove home I don't know. Tears were pouring down my face and I was hyperventilating. I remember coming home to find Carl in the backyard watering the garden.

When Carl saw my face he said, "Honey, what's wrong?"

"Talk to your baby Carl, I think I scared him. Tell the baby he's okay," I babbled as I headed into the bedroom from the patio.

We lay down on the bed together and Carl leaned down over my belly and softly spoke to the rounded form of my flesh, "Mommy's okay little one. Everything is going to be okay."

I just lay there crying uncontrollably. I wasn't okay and Carl didn't know how to console me. When he got up to check on the children in the other room, I locked myself in the bathroom. I heard the phone ring. Carl stood outside the bathroom door.

"Kathy? Honey, Joanna is on the phone. She just wanted to make sure you got home all right. Do you want to talk to her?"

"No," I replied through the closed door.

I remember leaning against the bathroom wall, then sliding down into a squatting position on the floor, inconsolable. Feelings from the memory flooded my soul like battery acid on an open wound. I could hear the muffled sounds of Carl on the phone, and feel my soul separating from my body. I felt like I was going to die right there with my baby inside me.

With a silent scream I cried out to God, "Help me God, I can't take it anymore. Help me. I'm going to die. God help me!"

Then I heard the soft voice of Jesus for the first time. He very clearly said, "All you have to do is turn, and give it all to me."

It was an all or nothing proposition. Could I trust Him? Would He hurt me? Would He save me? Trusting was the hardest thing He could have asked me to do in that moment, but it was essential. I surrendered to God entirely, holding nothing back. For the first time, I had to trust Him without reservation. I imagined handing God my heart, my mind, my body, and my soul. I gave Him everything I was feeling. For a split second I thought, "This is it, life or death."

Like water draining from the bathtub, the feelings of horror slipped away gently, and I felt a growing sense of peace come over me. I got up from the floor and turned on the shower. As I stepped into the warm water it felt like the Lord Himself was refreshing me and washing me clean. I was eternally changed in those brief moments by the touch of God's grace and mercy, precisely at the point of my deepest need.

Pain was the crucible from which my faith was formed. It was no longer an intellectual exercise or a philosophical platitude. It was the literal difference between life and death for me.

Though my father and mother forsake me, the Lord will receive me. (Psalm 27:10)

Chapter 11

Pandora's Box

The pictures of that first satanic memory haunted me day and night. I couldn't get them out of my head. When I met Joanna again she suggested I get them on paper by drawing them. With all of the talent of a four year old, I drew the images looping through my brain until they stopped. There was no way to capture the fear with crayons. There was no way to make sense of the black hooded figures, the blood, or the rape. But I was finally able to put the images down and let them go.

Joanna was troubled with the content of this memory too. She expressed concern that it was an indication of something more sinister than incest.

"Kathy," she said, "I want you to be very careful whom you discuss this memory with. Do not discuss it with your extended family until we know who is involved and what we are dealing with here."

One of the things she mentioned was the fact that memories sometimes surface on or near the anniversary dates of the trauma. August 3 was a satanic holiday known as Satanic Revels. She said, "What you described in that memory was consistent with reports of satanic ritual abuse (SRA)."

I had only heard the term "satanic ritual abuse" on a talk show once. I knew nothing about it. Joanna was fresh out of college and I was her first client presenting this type of memory. We realized we were both in uncharted territory and the learning curve would be steep. This one memory literally took the lid off Pandora's box in my mind, and there was no way to return without knowing.

The foundation of my identity was rocked to the core. God knew I needed to trust Him and to trust Joanna before I could step any further into the unknown darkness. She was the only person who promised she would never reject me. Joanna said she would see me through whatever was ahead, and I believed her. She became a rock for me. She was Jesus with skin on, a safe place in a violent storm.

Six weeks later on a Friday afternoon, I was at the checkout stand in the grocery store with Marie on one hip and a child from my daycare sitting in the cart beside me. The first mighty contraction came. I must have groaned. The clerk's eyes opened wide and her mouth dropped open.

"Don't have your baby here!" she exclaimed.

I smiled, "Oh don't worry. My baby isn't due for a couple of weeks yet."

But on my way out to the car with the groceries another contraction came. "Uh oh," I thought, "maybe he's coming early." I returned to the house to find Carl home.

"Will you watch the children for a few minutes? I need to make a run to Taco Bell."

Knowing they wouldn't let me eat in the hospital I stood in line for twenty minutes, counting contractions while waiting for my Burrito Supreme.

Our son Bradley was born twenty-five hours later by cesarean section, the day before his grandfather's birthday, on Fall Equinox.

Joanna met us at the hospital and congratulated us on our healthy baby boy. Lee was so excited when he heard the news that he rode his bike nearly ten miles to the hospital so he could see the baby right away. Marie wasn't sure what to think at first. She was only eighteen months old, but she didn't hesitate to crawl into bed next to mom and her new baby brother to suck her thumb.

Recovery was challenging with two in diapers and the months of sleep deprivation that followed the birth of a new baby. Carl and I had only been married two years and I was now mom to four kids, with the additional responsibility of a home-based daycare. The days blurred one into another and the memories continued coming without reprieve. I learned to recognize the approach of a memory by the sensory or emotional symptoms that presented themselves, and then accelerated until the entire incident was revealed. Sometimes anger came up, seemingly from out of nowhere.

On a summer afternoon in particular, I remember calling Carl at work saying, "Honey, this is an emergency. I need you to come home and take care of the kids for a while, I feel like I am going to explode."

Carl raced home from work, packed our two little ones and three daycare children and took them all to the park. Once alone in the house, the dam inside me broke. Somehow I had to get the anger out. In the garage I found a baseball bat belonging to one of our older boys and proceeded to swing at the couch in the living room screaming, "How could you do that to me?" "Why would you hurt your little girl?"

This went on for twenty minutes or more, long enough for me to break a sweat and feel blisters swelling on my hands. Then I heard a knock at the front door. I opened the door with the bat still in hand. Bryan's mom was standing there white as a sheet. "Where is my son?" she asked in a shaky voice.

"Oh my, you must have heard me pounding on the couch from the front door." She nodded her head.

"Don't worry," I said, "Your little boy is at the park with my husband. He is perfectly safe and sound."

Her cheeks flushed and then it occurred to me how worried this mother must be. We sat down together and I told her I was venting repressed anger from a memory. "It's the healthiest way I know how to get it out without having it leak all over other people."

She seemed to understand, and remarkably brought her son back to the daycare the following day.

We now had a term for the insanity in my life: satanic ritual abuse (SRA). Carl and I were insatiable looking for information to help us understand this strange new reality. We discovered, through The Cult Awareness Network in Chicago, that every major city across the country had reported incidents of SRA. They claimed most often it is multigenerational.

Joanna attended professional workshops on the subject and invited me to a local church meeting describing the dangers of the occult. We discovered there were many local therapists treating SRA survivors all over Silicon Valley. The entire area was a hotbed of occult activity, from San Francisco all the way through the Santa Cruz Mountains.

Subsequent satanic ritual memories surfaced with the faces of each of my half-siblings, my father, and my mother. They were all involved, and they all knew where we lived. I was terrified.

In January 1991, the worst in a series of memories presented. It was evening, and I was in Joanna's office on the couch, when my body felt like it was in labor again. Contractions came one after another, but I wasn't pregnant. My body was remembering. In my mind's eye I could see my bedroom in the Mountain View condominium. The shade was drawn and my mother was attending me. I was in bed, in labor, at twelve years old. With one final push a tiny, blue, baby boy was born, about seven months of gestation.

"Let me see the baby," I cried.

"No," she said firmly and whisked him away.

"I want to see my baby. My baby, I screamed. "Give me back my baby."

The next pictures were so horrific I could barely describe them to Joanna. I saw a stone altar and a stake driven through his tiny chest.

"She murdered my baby," I screamed. "Oh my God! My mother killed my baby."

I wailed in Joanna's arms uncontrollably.

Thus began a period of grieving for a loss I couldn't prove, for a death I couldn't explain, and the need for a memorial without a body to bury. The pain was so excruciating I could barely stand it. I cried all the time. I named my baby Christopher David and even wrote him a little poem, promising never to forget him again.

Carl didn't understand. "What do you mean you had a baby when you were twelve?"

"I remember giving birth. I remember my mother's face as clearly as if she were standing here. I saw her kill my baby," I cried.

"But you don't have any proof of that, right?" he replied.

"Right, I don't have any proof. I just know what I know. I know how I feel. I know how my body responded to the memory."

"That's just too farfetched for me to believe," he replied decidedly.

Carl called Joanna and her colleague for more information. Both corroborated my story. But Carl wouldn't believe it. I grieved alone, for a loss my husband couldn't understand. It was the first major misunderstanding in our relationship.

But God in His mercy acknowledged my loss in another way that deeply touched my heart. On February 3rd 1991, Carl and I dedicated Marie and Bradley to Jesus Christ at the nearby Bible church. The pastor gave me a rose for each baby. He gave me three roses. Then we publicly dedicated little Christopher to the Lord as well. That simple act of declaration and acknowledgement brought healing to my broken heart in such a tangible way. It was a precious gift to know my pastor believed me.

I attended church on a regular basis. The pastor and his wife got to know me a bit, then invited me to share my testimony in church one Sunday morning. It was the first time I was able to see how the Lord could use my pain to draw others to Himself. That morning another survivor of abuse stepped forward for salvation. I knew then the Lord wouldn't waste my pain and He had a heart for all those who have suffered. I began to view my recovery as a journey I was walking not just to be a better mother to my children, not just to break the cycle in my generations, but with a purpose to lead others in recovery by example.

This church embraced me. They stood beside me and loved me. It was here I also recall my most embarrassing moment. Bradley was about five months old. I brought him to church in the little white and blue sailor suit the pastor's wife had given as a gift. I was so proud of my beautiful baby boy. Before the service started I ran to the ladies room. When I was done, I put Bradley on my hip and walked down the aisle in my favorite blue dress looking for a seat near the front. Howls of laughter erupted behind me. I must have looked a bit puzzled.

Finally someone leaned over to me and said, "Your dress is in your pantyhose."

CHAPTER 12

No Safe Place

After recovering the memory about the satanic sacrifice of my first child, I no longer felt safe anywhere. At home I paced the floor at night, acutely aware that every member of my family knew where we lived. I was afraid to go to sleep, worried that they might somehow come and get my children or even me during the night. My greatest fear was that there could be a part of me that would go with the cult willingly.

"Carl," I asked cautiously, "I know this might sound strange to you, but I have to ask. I need you to make sure I don't leave the house at night, for any reason."

"What are you talking about?" he replied.

"I've been told that SRA survivors can get called back into the cult. That they use mind control programming and hypnosis on victims and all it takes is the sound of a bell, a phone call, or a special command to trigger the programming in victims to get them to cooperate. I don't want them to get me or our babies."

"Oh Kathy, don't be ridiculous. No one is coming to get you. You are out of your mind. Joanna is making you paranoid."

I took a deep breath and approached Carl with some facts. "Before Bradley was born my mother tried to get me to travel to Phoenix to visit. I was about seven months pregnant then, right?"

Carl nodded.

"Well, that's about how far along I think I was when the first baby was taken in that memory. It is exactly the time frame during my pregnancies with both Bradley and Marie that the insomnia and night terrors became so bad. I think there is a correlation. What if my mother would have killed Bradley?"

Carl's face was incredulous. He didn't know what to say.

"I know you think I'm crazy," I said sniffling, "but I am just asking you to keep a watch at night and not let me answer the phone or leave the house at night. Will you do that for me?" I asked.

"Yeah, alright, I'll make sure you are home at night honey."

"Okay, that's all I'm asking for," I said. But it wasn't all the reassurance I needed. It wasn't enough. I was living a nightmare seemingly alone, except for an hour or two during the week spent with Joanna.

I went to Target searching for a good deal on diapers, when I heard a familiar voice. I looked up in time to see my sister Tanya and her husband shopping a couple of rows away. My heart leaped into my throat. "Oh my God," I thought. "What if they saw me?"

I shoved my cart to the side, put a child on each hip and ran for the door. When I got home I was hysterical. There was no safe place.

"Carl, honey," I said emphatically. "We have to move."

"Move? Move where?" he replied knitting his brow.

"I don't know where. I just can't live like this in a constant state of terror," I said.

Our family of six was quite crowded in our little three-bedroom house, especially with the daycare. Carl agreed to search with me for a larger rental for our family. As we searched we realized we could not afford California real estate on our income. There was no way we could save fast enough to keep up with the rising cost to buy a house, and rental prices were exorbitant. We started a search for employment and affordable home prices out of state.

Meanwhile, my recovery continued. Nearly each appointment with Joanna brought with it another memory and a new revelation to grapple with. Pandora's box had snakes and spiders, bugs and coffins, and every form of perverse sexual abuse imaginable. I had been sodomized, used in orgies, and even had sex with animals. I recalled movie cameras in the living room as I was raped on the floor.

In an effort to erase my memory I clearly recall my father putting electrodes on my head and sending electric shock waves through my body repeatedly. Many memories included extreme acts of violence: whipping, stabbing, and blood-splattered robes. Drugs were used to paralyze my body and to silence me when I was conscious. I watched my perpetrators snort lines of cocaine, share joints, and shoot heroin.

With each memory came the task of pressing through the process. Denial was always my first reaction. "This can't be real. I must be crazy," I thought. Often I had to put the body pain, the feelings, and the pictures together to convince myself that they fit like puzzle pieces. Even in my wildest imagination I couldn't have come up with the horror sequences that my mind recovered. Once past the denial, rage would boil through every part of my body. My anger terrified me. I feared losing total control just by acknowledging it was there. But Joanna repeatedly encouraged me to get it out somehow, whether screaming in the car alone or using a punching bag in the garage. Over time, the anger became more manageable.

Beneath the anger was pain, an anguish of the soul so deep tears could do it no justice. Sometimes the pain became deep sadness and depression that lingered for weeks as I recovered one memory after another. I grieved the loss of my childhood and the death of my soul each time the past gripped me in horror.

Slowly, the healing came. A reclaiming of self began by acknowledging the truth and walking through the feelings. It was a full-time job demanding every ounce of emotional stamina and mental perseverance I could muster. I went to therapy at least twice a week and to the support group every Sunday evening.

Sometimes when I met Joanna, we would simply talk about the memories and feelings that had recently presented, processing as much as possible the work that had already been accomplished. Recovery took over every waking thought. I felt so crazy. But Joanna reassured me that I wasn't.

She said, "What happened to you is crazy, not you."

When I ran out of insurance coverage for the counseling, Joanna continued to see me. She knew she might never see the money, yet she continued to help me without compensation.

One of the most vivid memories I recalled with Joanna involved the abduction of a little boy I'll call Billy. I believe he was taken from the Oakland area just a few days before Halloween. The family put Billy in my care, so I watched over him like a big sister. He must have been about five years old, but I couldn't say for certain. He had a blue knit cap, blonde hair, and beautiful blue eyes. Because I looked after him for a few days, I felt responsible for him. When the Halloween ritual began in the dark behind the barn, Billy was there. They stripped him of his clothes, sodomized him, and while others held him down, the head warlock sacrificed him to Satan with a huge knife.

I screamed "NOOOOO!" Immediately they bound me, and threatened me if I didn't shut up.

Joanna asked, "What happened next?"

I replied, "All I see is white light."

"White light is good," she said, nodding her head.

The pictures of Billy ran through my mind until I committed them to paper and let them go. I don't know what happened to his little body, but I do know he is with Jesus now. I was devastated by his death, and felt horribly responsible.

Joanna said, "It wasn't your fault Kathy."

"But I should have known what they were going to do to him. I should have gotten him out of there," I cried.

"No. You were a child. You couldn't be expected to do those things," Joanna said holding my hand and looking deeply into my dripping eyes.

During the following session Joanna suggested we contact the police.

"Oh no, I couldn't do that," I replied terrified.

Joanna reassured me and then convinced me to do it. I finally agreed to speak with an officer if he was safe, and Joanna was there. She arranged to have him meet me during our next session.

I was deeply frightened. My husband didn't even believe me, how would a policeman believe me? The "don't tell" programming began going off in my head. "Don't say anything; people won't believe you and they will think you're crazy." Would this officer think I was a nut? It was one thing to tell Joanna about the memories as they came up, but it was something altogether different to tell an officer of the law. The act of telling became a bridge between the memory and reality. It took all of my courage to cross it.

At church, the day before meeting with the officer, a lovely woman offered me a needlepoint picture of Jesus with verses of Psalm 23 on it. She made it herself, and she said, "I believe the Lord wants you to have this."

I have kept this picture as a reminder that though I walk through the valley of death, I shall fear no evil, for He is with me.

I met with the officer on Monday. He was kind and gentle,

taking notes as I told him about the house on the hill and the hidden parking area off of the road. I described the barn and the place where the rituals took place. For the first time, I felt like an official was taking me seriously and it felt tremendously validating. I don't know what resulted from his investigation but I heard something about insufficient budget and manpower. It didn't matter to me. I spoke the truth and it is now on record. I thanked Joanna for arranging the visit with the policeman and we continued moving forward with our work.

The next memory to surface was beyond horrific. It began with a ride in the car in the middle of the night. We arrived at the town cemetery and gathered with the others in black hooded robes around a stone altar. They drugged me, and then placed me in a coffin. Buried alive, terror gripped me, but I couldn't move. I couldn't breathe. I couldn't scream "I'm going to die." The sound of dirt landing on the top of the box confirmed my death, or so I thought.

After some time, they opened the coffin and retrieved me. Standing over the open grave was Linda with a shovel, just staring at me.

A new boldness surfaced in my soul after that experience. I wanted evidence to substantiate what I remembered. This time I wanted proof it was real. I had to know I wasn't crazy and it really happened. So I drew a picture of the satanic altar, the headstones, and the surrounding area where this took place. I was certain to add a date on the paper to demonstrate that I drew the picture before I went to the scene of the crime. Then I went to the cemetery to see for myself the following day. I held up the drawing and it matched the outline of the headstones and the cement slab behind them. I held up the newspaper of the day and snapped pictures to match the drawing. It was all the proof I needed to press on.

In our next session I showed Joanna the drawing and the developed photographs. Concern etched her brow.

"Kathy I don't ever want you to go back to these places. You don't know what kind of danger you could have put yourself in," she scolded.

"But I needed proof. None of this makes any sense otherwise," I replied.

"I know," she said. "It's understandable at this point that you need something more than memory fragments to go on, but promise me you won't do something like that again alone."

"I promise," I replied, feeling comforted by the fact that she really cared.

If memory recovery during the day wasn't enough, I also struggled with recurring nightmares. In one such dream I attended a party in a big beautiful house somewhere in a Spanish or Portuguese-speaking country. In the dream I joined several little girls dressed in pretty lacy party dresses wearing black patent leather shoes and white lacy socks. We were climbing the stairs inside the house when a crowd of men with automatic machine guns burst through the front door and fired a spray of bullets. Every time I had that dream I woke up with a jolt. I told Joanna about it.

"It could be memory," she said gently.

Joanna had me focus on the feelings and pictures of the dream momentarily until the memory surfaced. It correlated precisely with the dream, with the exception of one important detail. I had been shot. Hot burning pain seared through my left leg. I don't know how I got to the hospital but in the next picture I could see my body being wheeled through a hallway and I was floating along the ceiling hovering over it. I looked so small on the big rolling bed. Was I dead or just asleep? I wondered. The nurses were shouting and running as they pushed the gurney through a set of double doors.

The pictures stopped and I felt my leg. There was a round hole in my upper left thigh that was throbbing with pain. "My mother lied to me!" I exclaimed, "She told me that was where I was vaccinated."

During a visit to the doctor sometime later, I asked her to specifically inspect the hole in my leg.

"Is it a vaccine site?" I asked, holding my breath.

She shook her head, "No, definitely not a vaccination. The hole is very deep."

"Could it be a bullet hole?" I asked.

"Yes, it certainly could," she answered.

I started bawling.

Tangible medical evidence confirmed that I wasn't crazy. I felt both relieved and sad at the same time. But the truth left me with many unanswered questions. What was I doing in another country? Why was I there as such a small child? Where were my parents?

Joanna told me she was assessing the level of trauma in the content of my memories and told me she was very concerned.

She said gently, "Usually with this level of trauma the personality develops something called 'ego states' or even separate personalities. Would you be willing to look inside and see if that is the case?"

I felt very uncomfortable with Joanna's idea. But I trusted her and was willing to explore the possibility. We found ten little girls inside that fit the definition of ego states. Joanna's voice was soft, but she continued to press, this time looking for separate personalities. I felt a very high level of anxiety and a struggle ensued inside me. Then one by one, different personalities stepped forward and introduced themselves to Joanna. It was like watching a movie where I could hear and see what was happening, but from a distance. I wasn't in control, another part of me was talking, feeling, and reacting. They had different names, different voices, and they were different ages. Some were very little, some were adults, but I discovered that each one was a part of me.

Once separate personalities broke through my consciousness, I went spinning out of control. Within weeks of that session I had two minor car accidents, and was an emotional wreck. Joanna encouraged me to stop doing daycare, but it was the only way I could support the family financially and be with my children.

Finally, Joanna insisted I consider hospitalization. She said, "There is a hospital not far from here that is very nice, it isn't a locked facility; they treat women who have suffered severe trauma."

With much prompting I finally agreed to go on the condition that Joanna continued to treat me. She agreed, and I closed the daycare and stopped nursing Bradley when he was eight months old. Carl drove me to the hospital and dropped me off. To this day I don't know what was going through his mind. Was he anxious, ashamed of me, worried? I don't know, and he didn't say. Hours after signing the registration papers, I discovered that a different doctor would be working with me, and Joanna wasn't allowed to treat me. I felt betrayed and trapped. One personality after the next stepped forward as though through a revolving door. Each peeked out and then stepped back for the next one to come forward. I sat sobbing on the bed, terrified, rocking back and forth. A nurse came in and tried to console me, but I wouldn't let her touch me.

Finally, a very strong personality stepped forward, packed my suitcase and I walked right out the front door. The staff and even some of the patients tried to stop me, but I was resolute in leaving. I found a pay phone on a nearby corner and called a taxi. Once safely in the taxi my heart stopped pounding and I calmed down. I wasn't sure where to go, but finally decided to go to the church for help.

My beloved pastor sat with me on a pew and said, "I don't understand why Jesus doesn't just heal you." He prayed for me, but I left feeling worse than when I came.

"Yeah," I wondered, "why doesn't Jesus just heal me? Doesn't he love me? Is there something wrong with me that he can't or worse yet, won't fix?"

I felt condemned and rejected. I went to a local bar and ordered a drink. I sat alone staring at the fireplace and the orange carpet thinking "now what should I do?" I didn't want to go home. I knew Carl would be angry with me. But by evening I finally relented and took a cab home.

"What are you doing here?" Carl asked in a frustrated tone of voice.

"I didn't feel safe there. I couldn't stay," I replied, drunk and crying.

He was disappointed that I didn't stay in the hospital long enough to get "fixed." It wasn't just his words but his body language that shunned me. I felt ashamed and crazy, terribly alone, and unsure of myself. I was falling apart and out of control, and my life partner rejected me.

In my quiet moments I pondered what it meant to have multiple personalities. Was I like the character "Sybil" from the movies? Or maybe I was worse. Maybe I was so crazy no one would ever want to be with me. Suicidal thoughts hovered around me like a vulture waiting for the taste of death. I wanted to die but I didn't want to leave my young children.

Joanna reminded me that my children needed their momma. Regardless of how I felt, she told me suicide would destroy my children's lives and set a precedent of death over them. She rattled off some statistics and convinced me suicide wasn't the answer. But the spirit of heaviness, like a black cloak, hung over me. I was living in despair.

Chapter 13

Rocky Mountains

We sat in the garage throwing darts at a map. "Where should we move?" Carl said. The dart hit Colorado. "Hey, I think I know someone who lives there."

Carl made contact with an old friend from high school living in Colorado Springs. After speaking with Rose on the phone, Carl was very enthusiastic about the possibility of moving there. Rose and her husband offered to let us stay with them for a few weeks while we looked for a place to live. This was the support we needed to make a long distance move.

Joanna was careful to tell me we needed to leave quietly and go into hiding. "Don't tell anyone where you are going," she advised. "And whatever you do, don't move to Boulder, it's a hotbed of satanic activity."

I was so excited I started packing right away. We planned our move for the end of June 1991. With the move eminent it was difficult to know what to say to friends, neighbors, and family without disclosing our plans. My mother called after our date was set, announcing she would be in town for a visit with her best friend Audrey. I didn't know what to say, but she was the last person I wanted to be aware of our move. So I told her to come visit, knowing we would be gone two days before she arrived.

I left California hoping to disappear, knowing I may never

see my brothers, their wives, nieces and nephews, or any of my friends again. It was painful. Every year since that day I have missed them terribly, especially at Thanksgiving. This decision was painful for Eddy and Lee too. Leaving all of their friends behind was hard for them.

We arrived in Colorado on the 4th of July. It was Lee's birthday and the end of a long road trip. Carl and Rose seemed to have so much to talk about. They sat up for hours reminiscing about high school. I noticed the look in Rose's eyes as she stared at my husband. It was then I realized they were more than friends in high school and she was still in love with him. I tried denying my jealousy, but every time I touched anything in Rose's house I broke it. Rose was good-natured about it, and Carl thought it was funny. But I was thoroughly embarrassed and couldn't wait to move into a place of our own.

We lived on the remains of Carl's 401k while he desperately looked for work. We thought he would have a new job in no time and we would be able to use the remaining funds to buy a house. But we went through that nest egg very quickly, and decided to rent a place first. We found a nice big home fourteen miles up Ute Pass in a tiny town called Mountain Park. Views of Pike's Peak and the Rocky Mountains were breathtaking from any vantage point in town. I thought it was the most beautiful place in the world. Our mountain home had a sun porch with big windows that faced south into the neighbor's field where his horses grazed all day. At night the stars lit up the skies above the mountains like diamonds on black velvet cloth.

Not long after we settled into our new home, Carl received a job offer from the Denver area, well over seventy miles away. We took a weekend drive to the area to investigate. We stopped at a local market and picked up the town newspaper. The price of housing was very affordable. Using the pay phone in front of the market, Carl called the first advertisement for a home that looked interesting. A woman answered the phone from Carl's hometown in Idaho. While they spoke she realized she knew him when he was a little boy. Carl was quite dismayed. She told him she was selling her home in Colorado to return to Idaho. Before concluding the conversation she invited us to come see her home in Gun Barrel Estates, near Boulder. The house was nice enough, nestled in a well-established neighborhood. She offered to sell us her home for a small down payment and we promised to think about it.

As we drove back to Mountain Park, Joanna's words rang in my head, "Whatever you do, don't move to Boulder, it's a hotbed of satanic activity."

It was hard to have an open mind about this opportunity as I watched the full moon rise in the sky above the freeway on our way home. I started crying, "I can't do this Carl. I can't move here. It's not safe."

Reluctantly he agreed and turned down both the job and the opportunity to buy the house. At first it seemed turning our back on that opportunity was the right decision. Just as our funds ran out, Carl found a job nearby. I opened a daycare in our home and it began to fill with children. I took a part-time job on the weekend and it looked like we were going to make it where we had settled. We put an offer in to buy the mountain home we had rented. The owner accepted the offer and it seemed our dreams were coming true. Our older boys were enrolled in school and began making friends right away. I found a little church nearby.

The first snow fell during the last week of August. Delighted, I ran outside to feel the soft, cold flakes melt on my tongue.

"Isn't this great?" I exclaimed.

My husband shook his head and said, "It may look pretty, but it's early yet for snow. It could be the sign of a rough winter."

Then one morning in early October, Carl came home from

work at 10:00 a.m. His face was ashen and serious. "Honey, what's wrong?" I asked.

"They just fired me. Just like that, with no warning, nothing." he exclaimed, choking back the tears.

"They can't do that," I cried in disbelief.

Carl sat hunched over on the bed. "In this state, they can," he said. "It's called a fire-at-will clause."

Incredulous I asked, "Why would they fire you?"

Carl replied, "It was something about a squabble between the owner and the general manager who claimed they were paying me too much."

One of the children in my daycare was the owner's son. The family removed their son from the daycare and in a single day all our plans changed. We scraped the last of our finances together to pay the rent for November. There was nothing left, and no work to be found. Coming from California we didn't realize work was primarily seasonal in this climate. Winter had set in. Within weeks the cupboards were bare, and utility companies threatened to disconnect services.

I remember a conversation with the water company clerk, "What do you mean you are going to shut off our water? We have four kids. You can't shut off our water," I said.

She replied, "Ma'am, we can, and we will disconnect your water if you don't pay the bill immediately."

I tried not to panic in front of the kids while I hung up the phone. All I knew to do was pray.

Jobs were scarce and employees were underpaid at that time in Colorado. Engineers were working for minimum wage and we realized we were in trouble. God was faithful though and He made a way of escape. We were able to get out of our offer to buy the rental house because it was contingent upon inspection, and the inspection report revealed numerous problems. The owner was satisfied with that excuse and we remained as renters.

It was about this time that our fourteen-month old son Bradley contracted a ferocious fever. His little body was burning up with a temperature spiking over 104 degrees. He cried and cried as I paced the floor trying to comfort him. We had no medical insurance, and no way to pay the doctor, but I called the clinic late that night anyway.

The doctor said, "Put him in a cold bath. When his temperature comes down to 102, call me again and I will meet you at the office."

A couple of hours later I put on my snow boots and put little Bradley in his car seat. He was nearly hoarse from hours of screaming. Carl stayed home with the rest of the children as I tried to get down the snow-glazed mountain with tires from California. I don't know who was crying more, Bradley or me when we arrived at the clinic. The doctor met us there and turned on the lights. I must have been a sight because the doctor fussed over me before he took care of my son. We left the clinic that night with a prescription for antibiotics. But I knew we didn't have the money to pay for them. By faith, I went to the pharmacy in the morning and asked for assistance anyway. The druggist filled the prescription as a charitable gift and Bradley quickly recovered.

Then came the day we didn't have anything to feed the kids for dinner. Remarkably, we were all invited over for spaghetti by a couple we had just met as friends. They had no way of knowing how desperate we were. But God made a way to feed us. The next morning I summoned my courage and drove downtown to the Ecumenical Society where I stood in line to ask for food.

A stern-looking gray-haired man looked over the card I filled out and then stared me right in the eye and asked, "You have a family of six?"

"Yes," I replied.

"And your husband has no work?"

"Yes that's right, not since October," I said.

"Well, you are destitute then," he replied, stamping my card.

I nearly choked on the thought. "Yes, I suppose we are," I said, with tears spilling down my cheeks.

Without saying much else, he loaded five sacks and a box of food into the trunk of my car and sent me on my way. I cried all the way home. Our teenagers must have known something was wrong; they knew we never bought ice cream in five-gallon containers and the packages in the cupboard were all unfamiliar. But they didn't say anything. Instead there was just an unspoken knowing between us.

Carl and I finally broke down and made an appointment with social services for food stamps. Our food stamp allotment arrived just in time for Thanksgiving. We had a terrific feast including five pies which we gobbled down like ravenous pigs.

Worried about the December rent, Carl contacted the landlord to determine how much leeway he could give us. Without mercy the landlord informed us we would be evicted after three days of nonpayment. We were desperate and nearly homeless with four kids and a foot of snow already on the ground.

I continued to pray. The little church congregation prayed, and finally things began to change for us. Carl put our van in the grocery store parking lot with a big sign on it that read, "For Sale." We sold it for a quarter of its value just in time to pay the December rent. With that we sighed in relief. The pastor gave us a bit of gas money, and a friend brought diapers and formula for the baby. Somehow, we even managed to keep the utilities on. But we knew we had to find a job and a new place to live within thirty days.

Carl got on the phone, calling the employment departments in different states to determine the location with the lowest unemployment rates and the best wages. He had been on the phone all afternoon when he came to me with his findings.

He said, "Kathy, unless you want to move to Minneapolis, we have three choices; Seattle, Portland, or Dallas."

I had no idea what to choose. I had never been to any of those cities. But Carl had been to Portland for a job interview when he graduated from technical college.

"It's really beautiful there Kathy," he said hopefully.

So, we decided on Portland. As a last resort, Carl called his adoptive father in Idaho and asked if he could help us finance the move. Leonard was a man of very humble means, but he sold his life insurance policy to meet our need.

With a new direction and a plan to get there, we had nothing left to do but wait for the end of the month to move. We played in the snow with the kids, relaxed, and enjoyed the beautiful winter days.

For Christmas we used a credit card from a store in California and had goodies shipped to us to put under the tree. We didn't have much, but it didn't matter. When Christmas day was over, the packing began.

I was invited to share my testimony at the little country church before we left. The Lord impressed upon my heart the scripture from Ephesians 5:11 *Have no fellowship with the unfruitful works of darkness, rather expose them.* That scripture became a glimpse into my life's calling. It was "rhema" tattooed on my heart.

The pastor was asleep in the front row, and most of the audience was yawning, but I shared my story as best I knew how just before we left the state.

On our last couple of days in Colorado, the sun came out and the snow melted just enough to bring a moving truck up the steep driveway to the house. We loaded the truck, said our goodbyes to the neighbors, and headed for Oregon. A snowstorm followed us from Colorado to Wyoming, but the road was clear ahead. I followed the moving truck in our little Mazda with Marie and Bradley in the backseat. Every now and then we stopped along the side of the road for a quick meal or to change a diaper. Then we hit the trail again. Carl had Eddy and Lee with him in the truck. I can only imagine the burping and tooting they did to entertain themselves on that fifteen hundred mile road trip. As the miles slipped by I wondered what it must have been like for the pioneers who traveled the Oregon Trail more than a hundred years before us. It was a long dusty trail with little of interest until we reached the Columbia River and followed it into the city of Portland.

The city was beautiful with tall buildings facing the river and bridges that seemed to stretch for miles. Carl said I was driving so closely behind him that he couldn't see the Mazda in his rearview mirror. I admit I was a little scared covering unfamiliar ground with so much traffic, and I didn't want to get separated.

We finally stopped in a small town about twenty miles west of Portland and piled out of the vehicles to stretch. We stayed in the cheapest place we could find. Accordingly, the motel didn't even have a phone in the room. So Carl took the newspaper and a pen to a phone booth across the street.

That night we rented the "red house" in a lovely suburban neighborhood. It had a modest kitchen, four bedrooms, and a generous backyard for the kids. It was within walking distance to a duck pond and swings, and not far from the amenities in town. Ideally located, we discovered God had placed us in a neighborhood offering the best schools in the state.

Our teenage sons were enrolled in school and I set out to find a job. I had been home with the children for three years, and now I was ready to go back to work. Carl and I had an agreement; as long as the children were under the age of five, one of us would work and the other stay home with the kids, primarily because we didn't trust anyone to watch them.

There were seventeen ads for telemarketers listed in the Sunday paper, and on our third day in the state I had secured a position. Carl stayed home with the children and I supported the family on little more than minimum wage. I sold long distance service over the phone to little old ladies in West Palm Beach, Florida, who were "entitled" to a discount. Six weeks later I had a better job – running a telemarketing department.

Marie's third birthday arrived two months after we settled in Oregon. I took birthday pictures of my little girl, in a lacy white dress and little red shoes, in the front yard under the creamy blossoms of a Magnolia tree. Little Bradley watched his sister smelling the flowers with his blue blanket in hand. Spring came early that year. The winter of Colorado was behind us. It felt like creation was celebrating a season of new life with us, and God's fingerprints were all over it.

Chapter 14

Living a Double Life

―⋆―

The years that followed our arrival in Oregon slipped together in my mind like watercolors. Eddy and Lee entered high school and were often gone with their friends. Marie and Bradley went to preschool and then elementary school in the blink of an eye. Carl was Mr. Mom looking after the kids while I was driven to climb the corporate ladder.

As I changed jobs or exhausted insurance benefits, counseling became a luxury on the remnants of my income. I found a counselor who saw me as a charity case once a month, but it wasn't enough. In August 1993, I remember sitting in his office crying.

He looked at me compassionately and said, "Kathy, I think you are grieving."

"I don't know about what. I just feel so sad, and I can't stop crying," I replied.

"Could this be the anniversary of a loss for you?" he asked gently.

"I don't know," I answered.

He saw me a few more times before passing me off to his intern who watched me writhe on the floor in anguish while I processed a memory and then concluded our session with "get-well soon" platitudes.

At a point of desperation I received a recommendation for a

therapist named Sonya. I was told she was both an SRA survivor and a Christian. Her office was clear across town on the other side of the river, but I would have driven to the moon for help. My insurance carrier approved ten sessions at a time, providing the first consistent resource for counseling I had since leaving Joanna in California.

Sonya was skilled and effective working with me, and I learned to trust her quickly. We met every week, then twice a week. I also joined her support group for SRA survivors. Memories flooded our sessions and she patiently sat with me as I walked through each one. There were times I left her office in such shambles that I would run to the ladies room and collapse on the floor sobbing until I could compose myself well enough to drive home. One personality after another came forward to tell Sonya their story. They were male and female, some were very young and others were older, each age-arrested at the time of the trauma. At the end of each hour I never knew what condition I would be in or what part of me would come out to get me home.

On one such occasion, I lost my balance in my shoes and couldn't walk without stumbling. I pressed the button for the elevator and waited impatiently. As I stepped inside I realized a little boy alter was forward and didn't know how to walk in my high-heel shoes. Worse, there were several minor car accidents because child alters came forward to drive.

Sonya tried to chronicle each personality that came forward, but many refused to identify themselves. She painstakingly made charts and asked questions to somehow organize the menagerie inside me, but I couldn't cooperate. Why?

One of the primary functions of satanic ritual abuse is to cause trauma-based dissociation for the purpose of the mind control programming of the victim. During rituals the programmer watches the eyes of the victim until they can see the mind has fragmented under torture. Then they call the new alter forward and give it a name by which it can later be identified, given instructions, and abused. How could my parts trust that Sonya wouldn't do the same thing?

I continued the work of recovery, but this time it felt different. It was as though I was living a double life. There was the life I knew every day between home and work, and the life I remembered in fragments on Mondays and Thursdays. They were incompatible. I could not talk about ritual abuse at work and my husband didn't want to talk about it at home. I self-medicated to hold back the pain and the memories. Alcohol was the friend I met every evening when I got home, and the comfort that helped me fall asleep at night.

After five years of being tobacco-free, I started smoking again. It began with a cigarette on a break, then another one at lunch. I tried to hide it from the children, but I'm sure they knew. I was a frantic wreck every night trying to put the little ones to bed so I could sneak out to the back patio and have a smoke once they were asleep. I was riddled with guilt and condemnation over the addiction and my declining emotional and spiritual health.

Despite my best efforts to manage my emotions, another horrific memory took me off course. I sat down in Sonya's office and described my emotional state. We used EMDR to pull the memory up from the subconscious mind. Immediately my physical body had all of the appearance of being in labor. Wave after wave of labor pain washed over me physically until finally the baby was born in my memory. Then it seemed another was born. It took several sessions to pull the full content forward. Week after week I visited Sonya to do memory work. This wasn't a single memory, but a double memory piggy-backed onto the first. There were two babies born, at different times, a male and a female, both sacrificed to Satan. I was inconsolable. Doubled over in grief I wailed and cried in her office.

Sonya put the presenting personality to sleep after each session and another personality came forward to enable me to function. This went on for two months.

I looked in the drawer of my desk and recognized two distinctly different handwriting styles on the file folders tucked neatly away. I thought, "If anyone had any idea I was a multiple I would probably lose my job." When I was done grieving, my primary personality was able to return to work.

One of my employees smiled at me. "Welcome back," She said with a warm embrace. You've been gone a long time and I missed you."

I was stunned by her comment. No one else seemed to notice, not even my husband. I felt uncovered and vulnerable. But she never said another word about it. I assumed she was a multiple too. It takes one to know one.

As a memorial, I planted three young fir trees in the mountains, one for each of my lost babies. I left my tears in the soil. There was something deeply healing for me in that act, one that enabled me to finally move forward.

In April of that year, memories of the Spring Equinox presented from the age of ten. I remember seeing a crucifix with a naked man nailed to it screaming.

"He's a defector," I heard. "This is what happens to those who betray Satan."

As for me, I was laid out like food for the locusts. The sound of chanting was a deafening buzzing in my ears. The air was charged with electricity and terror held back my screams.

The last pictures I saw were in the morning when I woke up in my own bed as though nothing had happened the night before.

Chapter 15

Distant Places

Memories of being taken to strange places for rituals complicated my understanding of the various affiliations and organizations with which my family was connected. How could so many people be involved and yet it seems no one knows?

My mother took me to a Catholic monastery where nuns walked the halls in black gowns and white head coverings. I could hear her high heels on the cold stone floors. She gripped my hand firmly while we walked through the building. The ritual took place in a large underground room with no light. Candles lit the pentagram on the floor. The faces of other frightened children spooked me. This was a black mass amid Latin chanting and strange laughter. Blood was spilled everywhere while children whimpered in terror.

I flashed back to my tears during mass on Sundays with my Aunt Ginny and Uncle Bernie. Many years later I remembered what I was never supposed to remember, travel to the Vatican. At the thought, a burst of adrenaline runs through me and I shudder even now. "They will probably kill me if I ever tell."

Travel to other countries became a pervasive theme in the next series of memories that surfaced. Over the course of years I was taken to numerous places; from San Francisco, to Las Vegas, to New York, LA, and cities in-between. Memories of the South American country of Brazil surfaced with regularity, adding intrigue to the process. I ranged in age from two to twelve in each scene that surfaced. I was in airports, and in dark seedy places where the men smelled of sweat and alcohol. I was an offering paraded in front of them in a long line of sniffling ragamuffins as part of a child prostitution ring.

In one scene I was older, maybe ten or twelve. A big fat man, with a dirty white tee shirt and a nasty cigar threw me on the floor in a dark and wet basement. Cases of guns lay open against the walls and were stacked in corners throughout the room. He shoved a long-nosed rifle inside me. I understood his words to mean, "I better keep my mouth shut." In those moments I didn't know whether I would live or die, and I thought, "If he pulls the trigger no one will ever find my naked body here."

Then he raped me.

I remembered being on a fishing boat, naked in a cage on the deck. The men spoke a language I didn't understand. I was young, maybe three or four years old. They poked me with sticks and treated me like an animal. Sea sick I vomited all over the floor of the cage to howls of ruckus laughter. My parents weren't anywhere that I could see. I didn't know if I would ever get home or if they would throw me overboard in the cage to drown. I had no idea where I was or where the ship was going. Then the pictures stopped.

I also recall going into dark buildings with my mother that had strange diamond shaped symbols posted on a sign over the doorway and on the walls. My mother took me there several times where I was paraded on the stage naked with other children and then handed over to a swarm of men for their sexual pleasure.

Questions pummeled my mind. How could she do that to me? Did they pay her? What did that say about me?

As I put the puzzle pieces together a larger picture developed.

I wondered, "How did my parents manage to buy the pagoda in the foothills and the fancy cars and trips when I was seven?" It couldn't have been on their salaries. Then it occurred to me, my father had a private pilot's license and he loved to fly. How did he finance all of this? Was he gun smuggling, drug smuggling, using me as the mule? Could there be that much money in kiddie porn?

I grieved again at the betrayal of being objectified and at the loss of my childhood. Clearly, money was more important than my safety. Why else would I have been to these places? Why else would my heart pound at the thought of walking through customs?

In the long litany of memories I recovered with Sonya, there is still one more worth mentioning. It took place in Connecticut. I may have been twenty years old at the time. In the ritual my first husband Jack and I had joined a coven of witches for a ceremony near the pond behind our house. To my horror, I realized I was leading part of the ceremony and I knew what I was doing. It broke my heart to remember. That was the oldest adult memory retrieved. Thankfully it was the only one.

This revelation certainly answered some questions. My father probably hand-picked Jack to be my handler and gave him responsibility over me. He was clearly a cult plant in my life, designed to keep me in bondage to Satan. The string of lights I saw behind the pond was no accident; they knew more about me than I did about them. The worst part was the realization that I had participated in rituals all the way into adulthood when I could have made other choices…, or could I? All Jack had to do was call forward an alter trained to serve the cult by using triggers and accessing my programming and I never would have known. The host of my system "Kathy" had no memory of this ever happening. What a brilliant cover. Raise cult slaves that are amnesic and access their hidden personalities without the host ever knowing.

I have wondered if this is what happens in those stories you hear on the news when the neighbors say, "He was such a nice man. We can't believe he would ever murder anyone."

Dr. Jekyll and Mr. Hyde strike again.

In 1995, Sonya asked me to check inside to determine how many personalities we were working with. I thought, "Oh, maybe she is losing count." But when I checked I felt there were more than 400 personalities fragmented inside. The noise in my head was deafening. For the first time, I began to lose hope that I would ever be whole. Maybe it wasn't really possible to put Humpty Dumpty back together again.

There was no safe place in my childhood and there was no way to manage the feelings as an adult. It was all I could do to hold a job and support my family.

From the first ritual memory I recovered with Joanna to the last work I did with Sonya, I chronicled over 100 memories in about five years. The constant drama of memories and therapy wreaked havoc on my marriage with Carl. Every night when I came home he worried about what kind of "mood" I would be in. He hated therapy nights. We argued and yelled, even in front of the children.

Carl confronted me, "How do you know these aren't just false memories Sonya has planted in your head? I have half a mind to sue her for messing up our lives."

I tried to defend Joanna and Sonya, but it was no use. He wasn't hearing me. Then the worst betrayal happened. Carl threatened to leave me and take the kids.

He yelled, "Any court in the country would declare you crazy and an unfit mother. All they would have to do is pull your therapy records that say MPD."

Carl was right. I was awful to live with. My emotions were

constantly spilling all over the place. If anyone had taken even one look at my medical records, I wouldn't stand a chance in any court.

I just froze. Threatening to take my children, the only two that survived, was the worst betrayal I could imagine. At that point our marriage began to die, only seven years into it. I withdrew, harboring deep resentment against Carl. I made a resolution not to talk about what I was going through when I came home. I didn't care who I had to live with, or what I had to do to ensure that I would see my children every day. I learned to pretend at home. I drank to suppress my fears and calm my nerves. I ate to deny my feelings of anger and the pain I felt in our marriage. Carl never threatened again, and he didn't leave me physically; just emotionally.

Chapter 16

God Provides

Stress continued to mount in my life. Carl was home with the kids all day while I worked to support the family. I spoke to him once about quitting my job but he insisted I continue. On the job there was an underlying tone of sexual harassment all too familiar to me. I was sometimes shunned and ridiculed by the men on staff.

In a particularly upsetting incident, the sales manager said to me "If you don't shut your **** mouth I am going to shove my **** fist right down your throat!"

Several of my employees were standing there to witness it. I just walked out of the building and got in my car. The next thing I knew I was lost somewhere downtown. I didn't know where I was or how I got there. I had lost time. Someone else inside had taken the driver's seat as I cowered in the back of my mind, licking my wounds.

Later that day I returned to the office and my friend James said, "Wow, I didn't think you would ever come back. What he said to you was horrible."

I smiled, "I'm here to feed my children Cheerios."

He laughed with me as I nervously straightened my desk. I couldn't quit, it would give Carl one more reason to hate me and take my children, so I persevered another year on the job. During that year I spent a lot of time with James. He was a delightful friend and we had a lot of fun together, but he didn't really understand what I was going through.

Sometimes at lunch we would walk across the street to the mall and get Chinese takeout from the food court. On our way back through the mall, I recall walking past a frame shop where the hologram of a gun was hanging in the window. As we walked past, the gun appeared to move and I fell instantly on the floor, screaming hysterically.

James' response was "You thoroughly embarrassed me! I'm not going to the mall with you anymore."

By the end of that year, I felt like I was going to have a nervous breakdown. My boss brought me into his office with the new sales manager and made jokes about Vaseline in an obvious attempt to provoke me. I was so angry, I walked out. The next day I contacted an attorney and filed a complaint with the state. The entire management team was served notice for harassment, but they didn't take me seriously and the harassment continued. Finally I decided to approach Carl again on the subject of leaving the job.

I said, "I am quitting this job whether we end up on food stamps or not. I can't take it anymore. Maybe it's time you get your butt back out there and start working."

He didn't say much and was uncharacteristically passive about it. The next day I resigned and the boss walked me out the door with glee. My insurance ran out when the job ended and so did my ability to see Sonya for therapy. The complaint I filed with the state was closed due to lack of evidence. And after ten weeks of unemployment, Carl and I were facing financial ruin once again.

While making the bed one morning I remember thinking, "If every hair on my head is counted then God must check in every day, because I'm losing my hair by the handful." Then I wondered if He realized how gray it was getting under my last box of color. We had empty cupboards for a week while we waited for food stamps to arrive. Our grocery list was two pages long the day my husband chased the mailman through the neighborhood to get them.

Excited, we jumped in the car and drove to the market. Carl and I each grabbed a shopping cart and began loading them with necessities. I noticed Carl chatting with an elderly woman in the meat department. I smiled as I pushed my cart past them, heading for the dairy case. With Easter just a few days away, I inspected three cartons of eggs for my cart. When I looked up from the egg case I saw the same woman Carl had been speaking with standing beside me.

Feeling her eyes upon me I chuckled and said, "We have a large family, we go through a lot of eggs this time of year."

She gave me a warm, genuine smile, her eyes twinkling she said, "This is a lovely time of year."

We chatted for a moment. As she walked away I muttered, "Bless you."

She stopped and asked, "Are you a Christian?"

"Yes, yes I am," I replied.

She reached in her purse and handed me a devotional poem she had written and a twenty-dollar bill. "God told me to give this to you for your family," she said.

Dumbstruck, with tears in my eyes, I said "Thank you."

There was no way she could have known how desperately we needed that money for the things food stamps don't buy, like toilet paper, feminine products, and shampoo. She went on her way and I stood in the dairy section reading the poem she had given me, titled "Rose Sweet."

I waved to Carl. "Honey, you won't believe what just happened. The woman you were talking with a while ago just handed me this." I showed him the twenty-dollar bill.

Carl was moved. We hugged each other and I praised God

for His provision. A few minutes later, in the frozen foods section, we were standing together with our welling carts when this elderly woman approached us again.

"I see you're together, you must be a family," she said.

We introduced ourselves.

She said, "My name is Jane." Then she handed Carl a roll of bills. "This is all I have on me. But God told me to give this to you. He said you need it."

Carl uncurled the currency. There in his hand was another eighty dollars. We both wept openly in front of the ice cream case. I told Jane I had been unemployed for weeks and we had hit desperate times.

"I am on disability," she said. "But I had a little extra this month. You know, I wasn't feeling much like going shopping today, but the Lord told me there was a blessing here, so I came and I found you."

Carl's tears streamed down his cheeks, "Kathy, I didn't want to worry you, but there's something you should know. The checking account had three dollars in it this morning when I called the bank. But there are almost eighty dollars in checks that haven't come in yet. What she gave us will cover our account exactly."

That same afternoon I had a job interview. Before the close of the following week I received a confirmation of employment.

> *I have been young and now am old; yet I have not seen the righteous forsaken, nor his descendants begging bread. He is ever merciful...* (Psalm 37:25)

Chapter 17

Amends

A property manager offered me a job running executive suites. My first assignment was to learn about the business from the current tenant, then oust him from the building. I was so desperate I would have done just about anything.

"Okay," I said, "I'll take it."

After surveying the needs of the business I realized if I was successful rebuilding the business and filling the suites with tenants I could work my way out of a job within a year.

Marie was ready for 1st grade and Bradley was enjoying his last year of preschool. Carl left a part-time position as a school bus driver and went to work at an electronics company. Our oldest son Eddy was already out on his own and Lee was struggling in high school and in trouble with the law. I was focused on my new job, compulsive dieting, and exercise.

By early spring 1996, we finally qualified to buy our first home. We searched neighborhoods all over Portland and settled on a yellow split-level ranch in a cul-de-sac just two miles from the red house.

Marie celebrated her seventh birthday the day after we moved into our new house. Carl and I were so elated we could barely contain our joy. We were like little kids the day we took the keys. We bounced up and down the stairs and ran through the yard untamable. The first summer in our new home was glorious. The backyard was alive with flowers and birds. We had our own private park just outside the patio doors.

At Easter I felt a prompting to try the great big church that was just a few blocks down the street from our house. When I entered the building, there in the foyer was Jane.

She smiled at me, recognizing me from the market.

"Is this your church?" I asked.

"Yes," she said, "I've been attending for eighteen years now. I'm so happy to see you. Would you like to sit with me and my husband?"

Jane introduced me to her husband and I followed them to a pew near the front of the church. "Where's your husband?" Jane asked.

"Oh, he doesn't go to church," I replied feeling uneasy. "It's just me and the children. I have heard they have a good children's program here. Is that true?"

Jane reassured me it was one of the best in the state. After the service she introduced me to the senior pastor. His blue eyes pierced right through me as he shook my hand.

While Pastor Ron made his rounds, Jane whispered in my ear, "He's a bit of a celebrity you know. He writes books and has a radio program. He's really quite famous around here."

I smiled, "Oh, I've never heard of him before. But I really liked the message this morning. I'm sure I'll be back."

I walked home with Marie and Bradley pondering this divine encounter. God had placed me there for a reason. He probably knew I would try the closest church to the house. It felt like home from my very first visit. There was something different about this pastor's sermons. He spoke of the love of God, the tenderness of the Father, and the compassion of Jesus. I had never thought of God in that way before.

The God of my experience was demanding, a perfectionist,

angry, critical and judgmental, and always looking for a reason to punish me. But this new perspective on the God of love changed my life. I wanted to know this God. I wanted to know the Bible like other Christians and I wanted to become more like Jesus. Jane was just the person to disciple me.

We called each other frequently and I went to her home to help with chores from time to time. I called her Mama Jane, and she considered me her spiritual daughter. I grew to love and trust her deeply as the mother I never had and always wanted.

Mama Jane knew how to reach me. She encouraged me to put God first, to read the Word every day, and she taught me how to pray. We prayed for each other, and she prayed like a grandma for my children. There were times when she corrected me, and I was able to receive her wisdom by faith. For the first time in my life, I began to mature spiritually.

God was moving in my heart and life as never before when an unusual experience occurred repeatedly in the morning, just before I was fully conscious. I felt a tapping on my shoulder and heard the words, "It's time to put the cigarettes down Kathy."

At first I thought I was just nuts. But it happened again and again. I thought, "No, I'm not ready to quit smoking." Then I remembered what Kitty Katherine said to me in Connecticut just after I was saved, "You'll know you are really saved when you quit smoking."

I don't believe cigarettes are a matter of salvation; however, walking with God changes one's attitude and perspective on sinful habits. In this case the Holy Spirit was trying to get my attention on the matter. Consistently every morning, the tapping occurred until I finally gave in. I thought, "Okay God, if you want me to stop smoking, I need you to help me and take it away." I made a choice to be obedient, and trusted God to do the rest. The first few days of being tobacco-free was a challenge, but it got easier with time.

Then one morning as I was backing out of the driveway I hit Carl's car. Expletives flew out of my mouth and immediately I ran off to 7-Eleven to buy cigarettes.

When I walked into the office that morning my assistant said to me, "Hand 'em over."

"What are you talking about?" I replied with my best poker face.

"Give me the cigarettes," she demanded.

"How do you know I have any?" I answered coyly.

"Carl called before you got here and told me what happened this morning. He said you were really upset. I know you," she said. "Hand 'em over."

Sheepishly I pulled the package out of my purse and surrendered them to Catherine. "Thanks," I said. "You're a true friend." That was seventeen years ago, and I haven't had a cigarette since.

After a year of working for the executive suites, the prophecy I spoke over myself came to pass, and I worked myself out of the job. The business was finally turning a profit and all of the commercial suites had been rented. They didn't really need me at that point. I knew it was time to hand the reigns over to Catherine. My boss suggested I take over a shopping center project. I researched his idea, worked on a business plan, and then confessed I didn't think his idea would work due to competition. He promptly fired me.

This time I had a stronger faith to ride out the financial roller coaster that always came with job transitions. My next position was as the VP of a struggling software company in Vancouver. Again I wrote a business plan with the owner of the company. The board of directors agreed to the plan and I was off and running with the daily operations of this tiny little venture. On staff were just three of us: a software engineer, a technician, and me doing administration and sales in a lovely building downtown.

Autumn leaves were turning beautiful shades of red, orange, and gold when Pastor Ron began preaching a series called "The Tender Commandments" from which he published a book by the same name. He was a marvelous speaker and when he preached I felt like he was talking directly to me, although I sat among two thousand others in the sanctuary. The pastor's perspective on the commandments was quite unlike any I had ever known. He spoke of God's love in the rules and demonstrated God's desire for relationship within them. Every week the pastor gave a sermon on one of the commandments with an intro and conclusion spanning twelve weeks. As time passed I could see the fifth commandment coming – "Honor thy father and mother." It worried me. I wanted to please my Father in Heaven by obeying his commandments, but this one was a stumbling block.

After church on Sunday I realized the check I had written for the offering was still in my purse. So the next morning I planned to drop it off before heading to work. I pulled into the church parking lot and headed toward the church office when I ran into one of the other church pastors. Pastor Chuck stopped and smiled at me.

"What brings you to church so early on a Monday morning?" he asked.

I told him about the check and then felt compelled to ask him about the fifth commandment. "If your parents terribly abused you, how do you honor them?" I asked.

He gave me a reassuring smile and led me into the sanctuary to pray. He said "You honor them by forgiving them. You honor them by praying for them."

I told him my father died when I was nineteen but my

mother was still living somewhere in Arizona and I hadn't seen her in years.

"Let's pray for her," he suggested. Dutifully I bowed my head and we prayed for her salvation. Then I gave Pastor Chuck the check.

He said, "You know, it was no accident you came this morning."

That single event put hundreds of tiny events into motion.

During a Thursday night prayer meeting, Mama Jane sat next to me on the pew. She reached for my hand and said, "Come now, get on your knees with me. It is time for you to forgive your mother."

"I don't think I can forgive my mother," I replied.

"You need to forgive her, you will never be free unless you do so," Mama Jane insisted.

I got on my knees next to her on the floor, and she led me in a simple prayer. She draped a thin arm around me and let me cry.

"You'll feel better now," she said.

And I did.

Forgiveness is a process, for me it was a lengthy one. In my morning devotions the Holy Spirit sometimes brought to mind specific events for which I felt hurt and angry with my mother. He gently led me to surrender my bitterness, hatred, and resentment so He could fill me with more of Him. I learned to forgive her in prayer, by faith. After some progress had been made I felt the Lord prompting me to reconcile with my mother and tell her I had forgiven her personally. I chewed on the idea for a while. Finally I mustered some courage to make a call to Arizona and say those words to her. She was surprised to hear from me. I said, "I just wanted to let you know I forgive you."

"Oh," she replied, as though there was nothing to forgive her for. "Just a minute," she said.

I could hear Pappy's voice in the background. When my mother returned to the line she asked, "Where's my money?"

"What?" I said incredulous. "Your money?"

Carl and I had borrowed money from her before I was aware of the abuse. We repaid approximately a third of the loan, but stopped the payments when we "disappeared." I was speechless. Her words rubbed salt in a wound that told me I had no value as a person. I quickly ended the conversation and hung up the phone with no intention of contacting her again.

I decided to move on with my life and leave her far behind me. But the Holy Spirit wouldn't let me close that door. He was persistent. Once again, the Lord asked me to forgive my mother, only this time in person. "Oh no," I thought. "No way." I really dug in my heels on this one. After some insistence I finally told the Lord, "I'll go visit her, but you have to pave my way and make it happen."

In God's mercy He didn't strike me dead for speaking to Him that way. I think He was looking for the willingness in my heart with mercy in His.

CHAPTER 18

Trusting with Fear and Trembling

———•———

Listening to Pastor Ron on the radio, I sat on the Fremont Bridge stuck in morning traffic on my way to work in Vancouver. He was now on the seventh commandment from Exodus 20:14 – *Do not commit adultery.*

I remember thinking, "That's not an issue for me. I've always been faithful to my husband." So I changed the radio station. I felt the quickening of the Holy Spirit warning me not to fall into temptation. But the thought promptly drifted from my mind.

My days were long at the office. Many times it was just Dan the technical genius, and I, working together. He asked me questions about my life and was genuinely interested in how I felt. He wanted to know my story and I was a sucker for a listening ear. I didn't realize how starved I was for emotional intimacy and validation. The next thing I knew I was in his arms.

Dan lived on a boat in Janzen Beach on the Columbia River. He invited me over to show me his boat. It was really beautiful with warm wood and very simple décor. I noticed a little Buddha statue on the counter and realized this man was not a Christian. We talked and had drinks, then returned to the office.

Carl intuitively knew something was wrong. He called my pager, but I didn't return his call.

The team worked late that Friday night, so I decided to reward both employees with a dinner at the local diner. I called home and told Carl we were eating out and I would be home later.

As the food arrived, so did Carl and his son Eddy.

Carl punched Dan in the nose and hollered, "Get away from my wife."

I started screaming at Carl to get out. I followed him out to the parking lot and told him I wanted a divorce. He and Eddy left and Dan took me back to the office. I curled up in a little ball on the floor and sobbed. Dan just held me until I calmed down, then we returned to the boat.

That night Carl visited Mama Jane in tears. He didn't know what to do. She comforted him and assured him she would pray. Now when Mama Jane prayed, God moved heaven and earth for her. Jane later told me that she prayed for hours with all of the strength she had, and asked God to expose this man to me, so I would know the truth.

I was feeling guilty, and mentioned the Bible.

Dan said, "The Bible is just an old book of words. They are just words, Kathy they don't have any power."

The scripture from John 1:1 ran through my head, *In the beginning was the Word, and the Word was with God, and the Word was God.* I knew then I had two choices. If I stayed with Dan I could start a new life on the river and keep my job, but I would have to give up my family and my faith. Or, return to a man I no longer loved and my children whom I adored.

The next day I returned to an empty house. Carl had taken the children to the coast. I was alone with my sin and guilt. I drank myself to sleep that night.

In the morning Carl arrived home with the children and said, "Get dressed. We are going to church."

"I don't want to go to church," I replied.

"Come on, the kids and I will go with you this time."

Reluctantly I obliged. When I walked into the sanctuary I felt the presence of God confront me. I couldn't hold back my tears. Regardless of the opportunity for gratification with another man, I knew I couldn't give up my faith. God had seen me through so much already. I knew I wouldn't survive without Him. I also knew God wanted me to return to my family and repent. It was the right thing to do, but I didn't want to do it.

Carl said, "I want you back Kathy. I want our family to be together."

I shook my head. "How is this going to work? Could you ever forgive me for what I just did?"

"Yes," he replied. "We can start over again. I don't care what it takes," he wept. "We can't do this to our children."

Monday I had to face my responsibilities at work. I couldn't be left alone with Dan and keep my commitment to Carl or to God. Dan was vital to the organization, and I was easy to replace. So I resigned without notice, well aware I had just burned a career bridge.

Carl even went so far as to say he received Jesus and had a public baptism at the church. He previously had a recurrent health problem, and was miraculously healed in the water. Carl began faithfully attending church with me and the children. I was elated and so was Mama Jane; we had been praying for Carl's salvation for years.

On January 9, 1997, I was cleaning the garage when I heard the Holy Spirit whisper, "If you will give up alcohol Kathy, I will restore your marriage."

I believed the Lord to be faithful in His word to me and I stopped drinking that day. It was the beginning of nearly ten years of abstinence from alcohol for me.

Our marriage dysfunction wasn't hard to determine. Carl and I were excruciatingly co-dependent and we were living in reversed marriage roles. I wore the pants in the family and was the primary wage earner. Carl worked menial jobs and took care of the children. In many ways I felt cheated out of being a "mother" to my children, they had learned to go to dad for emotional support.

Once again the Holy Spirit clearly spoke to my heart. I was instructed not to get another job until Carl had one first. I thought, "What do you expect me to do in the meantime?"

He answered, "Be still and know that I am God." (Psalm 46:10)

I waited while Carl pounded the pavement and sent out resumes. It took him six weeks to get a full-time job at a starting wage. Meanwhile I watched the bills pile up and once again we lost our financial footing. As soon as Carl was working full time, I accepted temporary work until I could secure a management position, but temporary pay was nominal and insufficient to cover the mortgage. By May we had missed four mortgage payments and were staring bankruptcy in the face. "This is the price my family paid for my sin," I thought, punishing myself mercilessly in the confines of my mind.

It was a warm Sunday afternoon and Carl and the kids were off somewhere and I was alone in the house. I got on my knees, kneeling over the green ottoman as my makeshift altar in front of the big living room windows. I thanked God for the time He had given us in our home and I prayed. "Lord this house was a gift from you, and you have every right to take it away. I commit it to you Lord. I surrender it back to you." In my hand were two cover letters for management positions I had applied for that day. I laid them on the altar. "Lord, this is your house. If it is your will that we stay here, I am asking for one of these two jobs by Friday this week. If the house is repossessed, please provide another place for us to live."

A bankruptcy hearing was scheduled in a week, and unless we could prove our ability to pay the mortgage, they would take our home in court. I knelt there and wept. I confessed every failure to the Lord. My sin had put the family in this situation and there was nothing more I could do to fix it now. I knew I had been forgiven, but the consequences of the choices I had made were nearly unbearable. Praying, I walked through every room of the house claiming it for Jesus Christ. Then I left it in His hands. There was nothing more I could do.

The next morning I received a phone call to interview for one of those jobs. The interview was scheduled for Tuesday. I pulled out my best suit and prepared for the meeting. Since I stopped drinking four months earlier I had gained weight, substituting sugar for alcohol, and a bag of fruit loops for a beer. My face erupted in full-blown adult acne. I was uncomfortable in my own skin. Before the interview I prayed and asked God for words. I had no idea how to explain the way I left my previous position, so when asked I skirted the issue. The interview went well and they invited me back for a second interview on Thursday.

On Friday Erica called. She was the head of Operations at Audio Visual View. She had spoken to the owner at my previous position and pointedly asked for my side of the story. I nearly choked on my words.

Carl overheard part of the conversation and slipped out the front door. Erica was silent for a moment on the phone. My heart was pounding and my palms were sweaty. There was so much at stake. "It will be a miracle if they hire me now," I thought, preparing for the worst.

Erica said, "I can't explain it, but I have a good feeling about you. I am prepared to offer you the position on the condition it doesn't happen again here."

I assured her it wouldn't and thanked her profusely. I ran out of the house to tell Carl the good news. I found him lying in the back of the family van, sick with worry.

God answered my prayer.

I started work the following Monday. On my second day, Carl and I were scheduled in bankruptcy court. Audio Visual View had provided me with a statement of employment and wages. I prayed it would be enough to satisfy the judge. Every nerve in my body was jumping. It was all I could do not to hyperventilate as we faced our creditors and the judge. When it was over, I cried with relief. The van was repossessed, but we were able to keep the house.

Immediately following the court proceedings Audio Visual View had scheduled me to be in Wilsonville for a vendor meeting. I was supposed to represent the company with its largest manufacturer. I remember holding onto Carl, saying, "I can't do it. I can't go Carl."

He gently wiped the tears from my face, "Yes, you can. You can make that meeting. No one has to know what you've been through today. It's okay. You can do it."

I refreshed my make-up and pulled into the manufacturer's parking lot twenty minutes late. I had no idea where to go. I walked around looking lost until some sweet soul ushered me into the back of a room packed with people. I grabbed a Diet Pepsi from the table and found a seat. I took a good long drink and settled myself in my chair. Then the unthinkable happened, "Urggh!" A great big burp gurgled up from deep down in my belly! Every head turned to look at me. What a way to break the ice. I could have just died of embarrassment. The lady next to me couldn't contain her giggles while I had to introduce myself as the new manager at Audio Visual View. It was an unforgettable entrance into the industry.

Work was challenging and demanding, but I loved this new position and threw myself into it wholeheartedly. It seemed the family was getting back on track and moving forward. Marie sometimes came to the office with me on weekends to help me put together decorations and sales promotions. The family came to the office for potlucks and parties. The company even loaned me the money to buy a used car. I was deeply grateful for the way they supported me and embraced my family.

In September 1997, Carl and I renewed our vows in a private little ceremony at the church. It was a simple service, but it meant the world to me. These marriage vows were consecrated to Almighty God and we committed to look to Jesus as the head of our home. This time we vowed to put each other's concerns above our own as we stared deeply into each other's eyes. Marie and Bradley stood beside us as the pastor blessed our marriage and our family. I believed that day God had truly answered my prayer and given me the husband I always wanted in Carl. We went to church together, we prayed together, and the children attended Sunday school where they both received Christ as their Savior.

On the outside everything looked good. But in the hidden places of my heart I was privately battling with compulsive overeating and bulimic behavior. I was so secretive about it that Carl didn't even know. I went from one counselor to another trying to find relief. Each counselor led me back to ritual abuse memories, but I preferred to live in denial, complaining that the issue was an eating disorder not more memories. Consequently I didn't get well. I stuffed all of my feelings, and repressed the memories with food and vomiting. I remember lying naked on the bathroom floor hugging the porcelain throne for the fourth time that day. I knew I needed help. I cried out to God, but no ethereal voice replied. So I hid alone in my shame.

At work I could forget my troubles, and busy with meetings and reports, I escaped. One of my favorite aspects of the job description was employee development. Audio Visual View hired an organization to come in and assist me with sales and customer service training for which I had a strong passion.

"Kathy, why don't you come to one of our sales manager training events as my guest," Ken said.

"Oh, I would love to accept your invitation," I replied. "Where is it being held?"

Ken smiled, "Phoenix, Arizona. We would love for you to have a chance to meet the president of our company, he is the keynote speaker."

"In Phoenix?" I said. "Well, I'll have to ask my boss and get back with you."

Audio Visual View paid for my flight and accommodations. All I had to do was show up for the free training seminar.

Wide eyed, I unpacked in the most beautiful hotel room I had ever seen. Then I went downstairs to the hotel restaurant for a bite of lunch.

After my meal the waitress returned with my debit card, "I'm sorry Ma'am, your card has been declined."

"There must be some kind of mistake," I replied flustered and embarrassed. I didn't have $5 dollars cash and no credit cards as a lingering result of our bankruptcy. I was stuck 1200 miles from home without any money. I wondered if Carl had enough for the children back home. Panicked I thought they would make me wash dishes or something.

The waitress gracefully noted my distress and told me not to worry about the meal.

I went up to my room to call the bank for an explanation. It turned out a six-dollar purchase had been keyed into my account as 600 dollars, which overdrew my balance and left me stranded. I was told it would be cleared up in a day or two.

The next phone call was harder to make. I called directory assistance for my mother's phone number. I knew God was serious about this forgiveness thing and I intended to follow through on my commitment to Him.

The phone rang while my heart pounded in my chest.

"Hello?"

I recognized my mother's voice. "Mom, I'm in Phoenix, and I was wondering if you would like to come see me? I'm staying at the Ritz Carlton for a couple of days."

"Kathy, is that you?"

"Yes. I'm sorry it has been such a long time since we have spoken. I was wondering if we could get together while I'm in town."

"Oh no," she replied. "I can't drive."

"Why can't you drive?" I asked.

"Well, Pappy died about three weeks ago and I'm on some medication. Please come out to Mesa and see me."

"Mom, I don't have a car. I don't know. Well, maybe I can take the bus or something." I told her I was expected back at the training session, but promised to get out to Mesa to see her.

I was haunted by her voice and the news about my stepfather's death. My mind wandered in the training session and I remember praying, "Lord, what do you want me to do? I have no way to rent a car and I'm not sure I have enough change to take the bus. You brought me all the way out here and now I'm stuck. I'm not going to beg anyone for money and I'm not asking for a ride. You have to do something."

At the close of the afternoon training session the gentleman who invited me approached and asked, "Kathy do you have everything you need? Transportation?"

I'm sure the fact that my jaw dropped startled him. I said "Well, as a matter of fact, I need transportation out to Mesa tonight. I was hoping to go see my mother."

"Stay right here," he replied. "I'll be right back."

Within minutes he returned with the owner and developer of the training program. We shook hands and he said, "I understand you need some transportation, would you like to come with me to my place? I have an extra car you can borrow for the evening. When you are finished with it just leave it with the valet at the hotel."

"That would be wonderful," I replied. "Thank you."

On the way to his house he told me he was a Christian and he somehow felt like he could trust me. I tried to conceal my enthusiasm as he handed me the keys to a pretty little convertible Mercedes. I thanked him politely and eased the car from his garage before heading toward the freeway. God had done it again. He heard my prayer, as insolent as it was, and answered it in grand style.

I cranked up the radio and stepped on the gas. I had never driven such a beautiful car. A bundle of nerves, I was hardly able to breathe as I approached the exit for Mesa. "What am I going to say? What is she going to say?" Worries tumbled through my mind like laundry. Then the Holy Spirit reminded me that I was now the daughter of the Most High God, the King of Kings, and Lord of Lords. I realized my relationship with my Heavenly Father makes me a princess. It is fitting for the King's daughter to be provided for so handsomely I thought.

When I found the address, my mother came right out to the driveway. She had been waiting at the window and saw me pull up. She was very impressed with the car, and mentioned the hotel. I think she assumed I had become wealthy, when in fact the King of Glory had adopted me.

She showed me her home and we nervously chatted for a bit. She had aged in the nine years since I had seen her. Her hair had gone entirely white, and the wrinkles about her face had cut deep furrows, especially around her eyes. I was terribly uncomfortable and unsure how to answer her questions.

"How do you like Colorado?" she asked pointedly.

"Oh, it's just fine, a beautiful state," I responded. It was clear she somehow thought we still lived there.

"I hired a private investigator to find you," she said.

"Oh, I see. What did he tell you?" I asked.

Her voice trailed off in my mind as she described the investigation of a woman in Denver that had gone on for all those years.

For a moment I flashed back to the job Carl turned down in Denver and the collapse of our dreams in Mountain Park, Colorado. Through all that suffering I now realized God had spared us.

I was tempted to show her pictures of her grandchildren, but resisted, careful not to give her any information she could use in rituals or forward to the cult. After a long awkward pause, I said "Mom, I want you to know I forgive you."

She had a puzzled look on her face and replied, "Oh really, for what?"

The Holy Spirit quickly put a hand over my mouth and in a flash He spoke to my heart, "She doesn't remember. She's a multiple who was abused just like you were."

I changed the subject and thanked her for her time. I agreed to return the next day, and take her out for dinner. She started crying, but I tried to reassure her as I left, feeling a new sense of compassion for her grief and pain.

On my way back to the hotel I pondered her comments. Something was not "right" with her, but I couldn't put my finger on it.

The next day the funds in my checking account had been released for use and I was able to rent a car for another trip to Mesa that evening. Spending time with my mother was very difficult for me. I reminded myself of God's promises of protection. I knew there was no safer place than in the center of His will, but that didn't make it easy. At every turn He had gone before me and come behind me with provision.

My mother and I drove to downtown Tempe for dinner at a nice Mexican restaurant. Mom was surprised at my refusal to drink alcohol, but indulged herself in a big blue libation.

We talked briefly about Pappy's death and what her life would be like now that he was gone. She seemed deeply sad, not just about the loss of her husband of twenty-three years, but I also sensed deep grief about her life in general. Tears welled in her eyes and she seemed to know I would step out of her life again, maybe for a long time. The small talk couldn't bridge the years or the memories. I felt compassion and deep forgiveness, but I didn't feel safe around her. After dinner I took her home and returned to the hotel.

The next day I tried with food to smother the myriad of feelings pounding through my veins. I felt I could cry for days, but I didn't want to. Any high-sugar content item I could find made its way to my mouth and I binged all the way back to Portland.

Once home, I was incredibly relieved that the trip was over and I had done what I felt the Lord had asked me to do. What I didn't know was that this was just the beginning of God's amazing plan to provide for us both.

Two months later, in July, Carl and I were driving home from a weeklong family trip to Lake Tahoe with the kids. We had been singing and laughing and playing games in the car on the long drive back to Portland. On the way we passed the "shoe tree" along the side of the road where people had fastened shoes to the branches of the tree. Of course we had to stop and add to the collection. We took pictures with the kids and commented on the novelty of it all. It was a tree of soles, reminding me of Psalm 1:3 *He shall be like a tree planted by the rivers of water that brings forth its fruit in its season, whose leaf also shall not wither; and whatever he does shall prosper.*

Not long after passing the "shoe tree," I said to Carl, "I feel like the Lord wants me to give my mother our address and phone number. I just feel it so strongly," I exclaimed.

Carl had an inquisitive look on his face. "Kathy, I've been feeling the same thing," he said. "I was wondering how you would feel about doing that. Your mother is getting up in years and she doesn't have anyone to look after her."

As I think back to that conversation I can only thank God that He placed that idea in both our hearts at the same time to confirm it so profoundly. I wouldn't have had the courage to comply without that confirmation. I found a card with a beautiful angel on it for my mother. In the card I provided our address and phone number and invited her to contact us. It was a huge leap of faith. We had sacrificed friends and family to leave California secretly and then became destitute in Colorado, nearly homeless with four kids, to finally find a place of safety for our family in Oregon. Sending this card would disclose our whereabouts to the most dangerous person in my life. I sent it in obedience.

Chapter 19

Mother

The battle with food raged on for me, so I scheduled another counseling appointment. When I saw the counselor he mentioned that my insurance company insisted I have a psychiatric evaluation. That was the last thing I wanted to do, but I had no choice if I wanted to continue to utilize the insurance benefits for counseling. It seemed to me they wanted to medicate me rather than pay for therapy. The childhood threat of a psychiatrist played in my mind and somehow the thought of seeing one was an admission of insanity. I remember praying and asking God to choose the doctor. Through some divine networking I heard about an old psychiatrist named Dr. Withop.

I entered his office feeling very guarded, just hoping to get the interview over with quickly. I told him I was a ritual abuse survivor and I was struggling with memories and eating disorders, but I didn't want any drugs. He looked at me and smiled.

With a slight German accent he said, "I have good news for you. First of all, I am a Christian and there aren't many Christian psychiatrists. Second, I believe satanic ritual abuse is real, although most of my colleagues would disagree with me."

He recommended a book called *The Antichrist and a Cup of Tea*. He jotted a note on his writing pad before looking up at me warmly.

"I think you will find the book very interesting. Next, I want you to call a pastor I know. His name is Paul. He offers prayers to reverse the rituals and has tremendous results. I think he can help you."

I wrote down his suggestions and prepared to leave. He stopped me and said, "Now, if the pain increases and you decide down the road you want some medication, you let me know. I'm here to help you."

I thanked him and scooted out the door greatly relieved. I don't know what he told my insurance company, but they paid my therapy bills and didn't ask any more questions. It took me several weeks to locate the book he recommended, it had to be specially ordered. When I picked it up at the bookstore I got some very strange looks from the clerk. But I was certain not to let that deter me. When I sat down to read it, my father's family name "Stuart" all but leaped off the page at me. "Stuart" was listed as an Illuminati family line.

When I was a child, I fondly remember my father's face light up when he spoke of our relations to Bonnie Prince Charlie and Mary Queen of Scotts. When I did a little ancestry research I discovered my grandfather emigrated directly from Scotland as an infant. And "Stuart" was dad's middle name, as well as the middle name of my oldest half-brother. I recall seeing the Stuart family crest and cloth. It was a source of great pride in my family.

This was an important piece of evidence, right there in black and white, affirming that my ancestors were occultists. It was a confirmation that I desperately needed to maintain any hope for sanity.

I thought of calling Pastor Paul, but I just couldn't muster the courage to try "ritual reversing" prayers. I wanted the eating disorder to stop, but every time I attempted to get treatment for it, ritual abuse memories came up. I didn't want to remember anymore. Every memory contained so much pain it aggravated the compulsion to eat. It was such a vicious cycle.

It was hard to find therapists with the best combination of skills needed to work with me. Some were experienced with eating disorders, but had no experience with MPD or dissociative disorders. One asked me if I would mind that he didn't believe in ritual abuse. Another had her PhD but didn't feel qualified to help me work through the trauma. Another wanted me to face each one of the little fragments of my soul and have each part draw pictures – there were so many kids inside I felt overwhelmed with the thought. Instead I binged, purged, and starved.

Meanwhile, our family continued to grow. Our son Lee and his girlfriend Emily gave us our first grandson in September 1998. Emily delivered Christopher just two days after Bradley's eighth birthday. We were all excited to have a new baby in the family, but it took me months to get used to the idea of being a grandmother at thirty-four. With the advent of a new child we all were given new names. Marie and Bradley became "Auntie Salsa" and "Uncle Bredy." Carl was called Papa, and Eddy became "Uncle Monkey." Family gatherings were filled with joy as we all doted on the new baby.

Just after Thanksgiving the phone rang in the early evening. "Hi, is this Rita's daughter?"

"Yes," I replied. "Who is this?"

"I'm Jennie, Rita's neighbor from across the street. I'm so glad I was able to reach you. I found a card in Rita's papers. It has an angel on it and your number inside. I hate to be the one to call and tell you this, but you need to come down here to Arizona and get your mother. She is in a really bad way."

I felt tension rise in my throat and asked what was going on.

She said, "Rita is losing things. She loses her keys almost every day. She hides her purse and then becomes hysterical because she can't find it. Yesterday she tucked copies of her husband's death certificate in her robe and was wandering down the street crying. I'm afraid if someone doesn't come do something she will end up hurting herself. I haven't heard her speak much of her family, are you her only child?"

I felt the weight of the world on my chest. "Yes, other than her elder brother in Detroit, I'm her only living relative."

"Well someone needs to do something. I think you need to come down here."

"Okay," I said cautiously. The wheels in my head where spinning out of control.

Jennie said, "Now, the first thing you need to do when you get here is take the car away from her. She shouldn't be driving. Then you need to get her to the psychiatrist."

By the time I put down the phone, all the color had drained from my face. "What's going on?" Carl asked drying his hands on a kitchen towel.

"That was a call from Jennie, a neighbor that lives near my mother in Arizona. She found that card we sent with our phone number and address. Jennie wants me to fly down there and take care of my mother. I don't want to do that."

Carl remained calm. "Honey, you are going to have to go down there. I know you don't want to do it. But, you really need to do it for her sake. You are really all she has left in the world. Isn't her brother nearly eighty?"

I met with my boss and told him about the situation on Monday. He said, "What do you need Kathy? Anything you need, you've got it."

"I just need a couple of weeks off to assess the situation and move my mother into a home or something."

"Done," he said.

The next thing I knew I was flying to Phoenix again, praying constantly under my breath for strength. I remember sitting next to a little boy who was traveling on the plane alone. He looked so scared. It was just like God to give me someone to comfort so I could get my mind off of my own troubles. When we landed I gathered my luggage and called a taxi.

The taxi pulled up in front of my mother's house late in the afternoon. Once again, she was waiting and watching from the window. I was nervous and didn't know what to expect when I got there.

She suggested we go out to her favorite restaurant for dinner. I agreed, and let her drive. We got a few blocks down Main Street in her beautiful new Crown Victoria when I realized she was driving twenty miles an hour on a busy thoroughfare.

"Pull over," I said firmly. "Rita, you need to pull over and let me drive, you're scaring me."

Jennie's words came back to me suddenly. That was the last time my mother drove a vehicle. After dinner we returned to her home and chatted for a while before turning in for the night. I tried to maintain some composure but wondered if my mother was aware of my emotional discomfort. She insisted I sleep in her bedroom.

"No Mom, that's your room. I can sleep in the other bedroom."

"No, sleep in my room," she stated adamantly.

What else could I do but comply? The prospect of spending the night under her roof, in her bedroom, couldn't have been more daunting for me. The house was so spooky in the dark. Much of the furniture I remembered from childhood, just the sight of it sent me into a time warp. I crawled into her bed feeling like I was five years old again, afraid of the dark. The house creaked and moaned like an old horror movie scene. I was just about to jump out of my skin when I decided to get up and get out of her room.

I went to the kitchen where I discovered mom sitting at the table. We sat and talked until nearly midnight. I don't even remember much of our conversation. But I do remember asking her if she would accept Jesus Christ as her personal Lord and Savior.

She started crying and said, "Yes."

I hugged her and we both cried. Her salvation was an answer to the prayer Pastor Chuck prayed with me almost two years earlier. Mother's decision for Jesus was made in some of her last lucid moments on earth. Awestruck by God's grace I realized He really loved my mother.

In the morning mother puttered about in the kitchen making breakfast. Intermittently she exclaimed, "They've done it again! They've taken my…"

"Who's taken your stuff Mom?" I asked.

She said, "The people under the house. They keep taking my things down there and not returning them. It makes me so **** mad."

After breakfast I strolled around the house. It was a single-level ranch, without a basement. There was no way anyone could get under the house. I thought maybe she had demons or maybe she was crazy. Something was definitely wrong.

Jennie came to visit and helped fill in some blanks for me. She had made an appointment for mom with a psychiatrist and I was to take her to the appointment right away. The stress meter in my brain went on full tilt. I was unfamiliar with the car and the city and felt like I hardly knew my mother, yet I was taking her across town to see a shrink. It was all I could do to focus on the road and avoid mom's questions. I realized once we found the doctor that mom had been there before. The psychiatrist said my mother needed to be in a "facility" and shouldn't be living alone. She also confirmed that she should not be driving. What she didn't tell me was mom's diagnosis.

The next step was a visit with a paralegal to obtain a "Power of Attorney" while mom was still capable of signing her own name. For twenty bucks we had two documents prepared giving me responsibility for my mother's assets and her health. It was all quite overwhelming to me.

Mom was appreciative of my help and very cooperative. But I knew I was turning her life upside down and I couldn't do it gently. The day came when I told her we had to sell the house. I put the house on the market with a realtor and asked mom if she wanted to come to Oregon and live near me, or stay in Arizona. She wanted to stay in Arizona.

"Okay," I said. "We need to find you another place to live."

I spent the next several days visiting care facilities and assisted-living centers. I found a beautiful place where mom could have her own apartment, but she wouldn't have to cook, and a nurse would supervise her medication and make sure she was okay. She could even keep her little dog "Cocoa" who was now elderly as well. The director of the facility met with us and after a brief interview concluded that mom was a good candidate for their accommodations.

Plans to move mother began immediately. I knew the sooner I had her settled, the sooner I could go home. We started packing the house right away. Somehow we had to whittle the items in a 2,000 square foot home down to the size of a one bedroom apartment. I put an ad in the paper for a garage sale and Jennie came to help me sort through piles of things.

In the office were stacks and stacks of sweepstakes forms. Mom had signed up for every sweepstake imaginable and believed she had actually won one of them. She was constantly under foot as Jennie and I tried to determine what needed to be done. Suddenly mother became furious ranting that she had a check for 3,000 from the sweepstakes that the bank had stolen from her and she wanted her money. That was the day I went to the bank.

After presenting my "Power of Attorney" to the teller, I asked for information on my mother's account.

The teller said, "Oh, I'm so glad someone came to do something about Rita. We were so worried about her. She's not right in the head, if you know what I mean. You see she came in here with some marketing slips from the Sweepstakes and believed they were real checks. We tried to tell her they weren't real checks but she just wouldn't believe us. She came in here every other day just ranting about the fact that she had made a deposit and we didn't credit her account. This happens sometimes with old people, you know. They get confused when they get things in the mail that say 'you may have won.' We were about ready to have social services come in to make her a ward of the state if something wasn't done soon."

I was taken aback. "What happens when someone becomes a ward of the state?" I asked.

"Well the state seizes all of their assets and puts them into a state institution for the rest of their days."

"Oh, I see," I replied.

I made arrangements to put my name on mother's checking account so I could manage her finances, and emptied the papers from her safety deposit box. The responsibility for her estate was overwhelming, but I pressed on, looking forward to the day I could go home.

The first day of the garage sale was a success. Neighbors came and helped price and carry things. All was good until mom became upset with people taking things from her house. She was confused and upset. I understood this was hard for her. I asked Jennie to take mom across the street to her house so we could finish for the day.

A moment later, I snapped. "Everybody go home," I demanded. "Come back tomorrow." "Everybody out," I started sobbing.

One of mom's neighbors put an arm around me and said,

MOTHER

"I was wondering how long you would be able to manage like this before it got to you too."

Once the house was quiet I fell on the mattress in Pappy's old bedroom and called home. I sobbed in Carl's ear for forty-five minutes. I had been away from home for nearly two weeks. I missed my children and my husband and I just wanted the nightmare to be over.

I rented a truck and began loading it with things for mom's new apartment. It took a couple of days to get her unpacked and set up in the new place. Mom was increasingly forgetful and emotional. I tried to be understanding and compassionate while at the same time earnestly attempting to get things done. We bought her a new TV to fit in the living room, and bar stools for the kitchen counter. Pictures went on the wall and it all seemed to come together nicely. Mother could walk to the community dining room for warm, nutritious meals and fellowship three times a day. She didn't have to worry about a thing. I also hired a lady to look after mom a few days a week by providing companionship and transportation as needed. It seemed mother was all set. I hugged her and kissed her and told her I would be calling to check on her when I got home to Oregon. Seventy-four years old, my mother stood by the apartment door with big tears rolling down her cheeks like a little girl as we said goodbye. It broke my heart.

I packed my things and did some last minute cleanup in the house before locking it up for good. Then I hit the trail to Oregon alone at 4:00 p.m. in the evening with a loaded eighteen-foot truck full of the things we didn't sell, and a diet soda.

After getting through rush-hour traffic in Phoenix, the road was wide open and clear for miles. I relaxed, put on some music, and prepared for a long drive home. I remember praying a prayer of thanksgiving for getting me through this experience and I asked the Lord to continue to build my faith. The miles stretched on and on when I finally crossed the California state line. It was nearing midnight as I drove through the pitch-black highway of the Mohave Desert. Then I saw a sign that indicated there wouldn't be any service stations for seventy miles. I looked at my gas gauge and realized the tank was nearly empty. It didn't occur to me to turn around.

"What if I run out of gas in the desert in the middle of the night?" I thought. A shot of adrenaline ran through me. I was scared. Mile after mile I watched the needle on the gas gauge drop a little further. "Oh God," I prayed, please keep me safe out here Lord. Don't let me run out of gas." Then I remembered my prayer about faith and wished I hadn't prayed it. Over and over I asked God to get me to a gas station before I hit empty. My palms were sweaty and my eyes strained in the dark for lights – anywhere that I might get help. Seventy miles later I pulled into a 24-hour gas station with the engine still running. The way that truck was sucking down the fuel I really didn't think I'd make it. But God did. He knew exactly how to stretch my faith. After a few hours of sleep in a grungy motel I hit the road again and reached a snow-covered pass in Southern Oregon during late afternoon the next day. I arrived in Portland just before the kids went to bed that night. There was nothing better than to hear their squeals when I walked through the door, finally home again.

Just as things were returning to normal at home, I received a call from Phoenix at work.

"Kathy?"

"Yes."

"This is the nurse at the assisted-living center where your mother is now. We are having a slight problem. Rita's little dog Cocoa is missing and she is very upset."

"Well," I replied, "That's understandable. She's had that dog for over seventeen years. But there is nothing I can do from over a thousand miles away."

"I understand. We just wanted to let you know what was going on."

"Thank you. I appreciate your time," I replied, before putting down the phone.

The next phone call was more distressing. Not only had they found the dog, but it was under the deck, dead. "How did it get down there?" I asked. "Mother's apartment is on the second floor."

The best guess from the facility director was that the dog either jumped over the patio fence or was pushed. It seemed to me the dog was too old and too small to jump the fence. Hmmm, I thought. That's very strange. I knew mom loved Cocoa.

Calls from Phoenix came daily after that. "She won't eat, she's depressed, she won't take her pills…" etc.

I kept thinking things would get better for mother once she settled into her new surroundings, but instead she was slipping fast.

I sent her a nice big basket of goodies for Christmas and called on Christmas Eve. She was severely depressed and I was concerned that she may be suicidal. After multiple attempts I finally reached her psychiatrist.

She said, "What do you want me to do? It is Christmas Eve and I am with my family."

Feeling impotent and responsible for her well-being, all I could do was worry. About six weeks after I moved mom into the apartment I received another distressing phone call. It was from the director of the facility.

"Kathy, your mother was seen chasing a delivery truck in her robe this morning about 4:30 a.m. She thought it was a lottery truck leaving with her winnings."

"You're not kidding, are you?" I said.

"I'm afraid not. Your mother needs to be in a locked facility. Her mental health has declined very rapidly since she has been here."

I realized it was time to bring mom to Oregon, but we had to find a place for her first. The pastor on duty at the facility suggested they hospitalize mother for ten days of observation in the psychiatric ward in Phoenix. During that time we could make arrangements for her in Oregon. I agreed to the hospitalization, then burst into tears as I hung up the phone.

Carl offered to help research nursing homes and care facilities right away. We didn't even know where to start. A couple of days later I spoke with the head nurse at St. Luke's and for the first time received a formal diagnosis.

"Your mother is a paranoid schizophrenic. She's depressed and has advanced Alzheimer's disease and dementia. She needs to be in a locked memory care facility. Will you be able to locate something like that before we release her?"

It felt like a bomb had gone off in my head.

"We've had to medicate her heavily. She is suspicious of her roommate and doesn't even remember her birth date. She does remember you, however."

Carl and I stood at the Portland International Airport waiting for her flight to arrive. I was so nervous I could barely stand still. Carl was anxious too. He'd only met my mother a couple of times, and he didn't know what to expect. A member of the flight crew wheeled mom through the gate in an airport wheelchair. She looked awful. Her hair was a mess, her clothes were disheveled and she was obviously disoriented. I took her straight to the ladies room to clean up.

"Rita," I said. "You're in Oregon. We're going to take care of you here. It's going to be okay."

The expression on her face changed from fear to anger. Afraid of her rage I changed the subject and got her out of the bathroom quickly. Carl and I wheeled her out to the car and belted her in for an hour-long drive to Salem where we had made arrangements for her to live in a beautiful new Alzheimer's care unit. She recognized the car immediately as her Crown

Victoria. Carl had gone to Arizona to pick it up just a couple of weeks earlier. We thought she might be happy to see it, but instead she was angry, frightened, and distrustful. She thought we had stolen her car.

Mom firmly gripped the seat belt and glanced about the car. It was pouring rain that day in January 1999. Then mom said, "There are balls falling from the sky."

Carl and I looked at each other and wondered what we had just gotten ourselves into. That was one of the longest most uncomfortable drives in memory. We pulled up in front of Altera, the brand new Alzheimer's facility in Salem. The director greeted us warmly and invited us to see mom's new room. She was terribly confused about her whereabouts. "Is this the Salem where the witches are?" she asked.

My eyebrows rose to meet my hairline. "No, Mom. I don't think so," I answered.

After completing the paperwork and walking her around, Carl and I left for home.

We tried to visit her every weekend and we brought her grandchildren to see her. Marie and Bradley didn't know what to think of this little white-haired lady who was so crazy. It wasn't long before they begged us not to drag them to Salem anymore.

For me, Salem was still a little too close for my comfort. Just the thought of having one of the most dangerous people in my life living in the same state as me was challenging. I comforted myself knowing that in some ways she was safe. Mom was nearly deaf and unable to use a telephone. She was now in a locked facility, so I didn't have to worry about her going anywhere. She couldn't see to read and no one in Arizona was given forwarding information to reach her. Essentially, she disappeared.

Chapter 20

Marionette Strings

I called Dr. Withop to ask him for any advice regarding my mother. I gave him her diagnosis and he said, "Have you called Pastor Paul yet?"

"No," I said softly.

"Well, give Pastor Paul a call and make an appointment. As for your mother, she is not going to get better, she will get worse. Just make sure she is in a good facility and well taken care of," he said.

It took a lot of courage for me to make the first appointment with Pastor Paul. I thought about canceling several times, but I showed up despite my trepidation.

His first question to me was, "Are you anorexic?"

I thought about what I was wearing that had given him that impression, a long navy blue dress tightly synched at the waist. I shrugged my shoulders. "Well, I may be a little bulimic."

Paul was warm and kind with his initial questions, interjecting his experience treating survivors every now and then as we got to know one another.

"Most of the ritual abuse survivors I've seen have eating disorders," he explained.

I didn't know what to say. It was affirming and upsetting to me at the same time.

Changing the subject, I showed Paul the book Dr. Withop

had recommended, and the page underlined denoting my father's family line as an occult family. When I told him I was also reportedly related to Dr. David Livingstone, he replied, "Satan has always gone after Godly bloodlines to destroy them."

Then he asked me if I had ever had deliverance from demons. The hair on the back of my neck stood on end and my stomach felt very queasy at the thought. "How would I know if I had demons?"

Paul sat back and reviewed my intake form. "When people are exposed to satanic rituals," he explained, "they can become infested with demons. What do you think they do in those rituals?" he said emphatically. "They conjure demons."

The wheels turned in my head and the pieces fell into place. I did remember seeing demons in my memories, but I didn't realize they had taken up residence in me. It was a horrifying thought. This wasn't something ever discussed at church, and my therapists certainly never talked about it with me.

"But I'm a Christian. Christians can't have demons can they?" I asked.

Paul said he could prove it to me if I would trust him for just a few minutes. I reluctantly agreed. Then he asked me to repeat a short Masonic renunciation prayer and called out the demon of the Stuart family line. I felt a writhing snake-like spirit rise from my spine and come spitting out of my mouth. It was unlike anything I had ever experienced in my life. It troubled me deeply, leaving me to wonder what else could be there. Deliverance was a path I had not taken in all the years of recovery work I had done, but I wanted to learn more.

I worked with Paul a couple of times a month. He seemed to know a lot about rituals and what to do to cancel their effects. For example, one of the first things we did was to conduct a spiritual divorce from Satan. I described the "Marriage to the

Beast" ritual when I was ten, which I recovered with Sonya in therapy a few years earlier.

It began with a stabbing pain in my left arm, an injection of some type of drug which left me feeling physically paralyzed, but my senses were alert and I knew what was happening to me. Naked, I was placed in a coffin that had been set in the living room. Inside the coffin were snakes and bugs as well as rotting flesh. When they closed the lid and began chanting, I couldn't move, and felt every slithering motion of the snakes and crawling bugs. I could hear talk of death. I couldn't breathe. I couldn't even scream.

Claustrophobic and hysterical, it seemed an eternity before they opened the lid and the drug began to wear off. I was "resurrected," then placed in a white dress and married to Satan.

Later that same evening, I recalled the cult doctor placing needles along my spine in rows and electricity shooting through the metal. I screamed in horror. Then he spoke words over me that burned like a hot branding iron into my soul, "You will never tell."

Paul shook his head. "I've heard similar stories before. I'm so sorry that happened to you Kathy," he said. "It's a miracle you survived." Paul looked down at the paper in front of him and wrote out a formal divorce decree that we both signed.

In a flash I remembered the diamond ring that had been used in that unholy marriage ceremony, and my mother had insisted I keep it. Paul explained that the cult curses jewelry in rituals, and recommended I get rid of the ring.

Inside I felt elation. The broken pieces of my heart thought they were forever trapped in bondage to Satan. My relationship with God instantly improved as though some invisible barrier had been removed, and I felt peace.

In a subsequent session Paul took a coffee filter and poured water through it, symbolizing the erasure of my name written in blood in the "Goat's Book." The Goat's Book, as I recalled, was a big black leather volume that was very heavy. All of the names written in it were penned in blood, including mine. I desperately wanted to believe what we were doing would make a difference, and the recovery process continued to take time and perseverance. As we made impact in one area, we discovered another.

Next Paul asked me about MK Ultra also known as Monarch Programming. It struck a chord of fear inside me. I told Paul about the memories I had previously uncovered involving hypnosis, mind control, bells, and symbols that triggered a desire to return to the Chinese pagoda. As he explained the programming, memory fragments began to fit together and make sense.

Paul explained, "Monarch programming is designed to draw the victim back to the cult in the same way Monarch butterflies return every year to Monterey, California."

I paused, thinking of how Monterey happened to be my mother's favorite place on earth. Every year she drove to the coast to see the return of the butterflies.

As I worked with Paul, more memories came up. I recalled the airplane hangars at Moffett Field where Lockheed was located. I was taken to the NASA facilities for medical testing and rituals. I remembered countless gynecological exams that finally culminated in the realization that they had attempted cloning, with me as the incubator. When the fetus died, the exams stopped. Who knew they were attempting human cloning in the 1970s?

Other than counseling sessions with Paul I had no place to process the trauma. I began to isolate and withdraw from people, and instead poured out my heart in spiral-bound notebooks, and my food down the toilet.

Paul asked if I recognized any people in the Rothschild family photos he presented. I wasn't certain, but I felt anxiety rising from the core of my gut and then I disassociated. During one counseling session Paul called out the "Legion" system. I coughed and hacked as the demons fled. Paul then showed me the passages in the gospels of Mark and Luke where Jesus cast out "Legion" from a demon-possessed man. In Mark 5:9 Jesus asked, "What is your name?" And he answered, saying, "My name is Legion; for we are many."

At full strength, a Roman legion was a well-organized group numbering 6,000 men. Could there have been that many demons in me? I was horrified.

But Mark 5:15 was a beacon of hope for me. *Then they came to Jesus, and saw the one who had been demon-possessed and had the legion, sitting and clothed and in his right mind.* I thought, "If Jesus can do that for the man from the Gadarenes, he could certainly do that for me."

Hebrews 13:8 says *Jesus Christ is the same yesterday, today and forever.* In my morning prayer I asked God for wholeness and to have a "right mind" every day. I persevered, and my faith grew. My mind was renewed reading the scriptures every day and slowly I was transformed.

In 1999, I attended my first 12-step recovery meeting for food addiction. I had to admit I was both a compulsive overeater and bulimic. Like everything else I had tried, it worked for a while, until I took my will back and buried my face in the refrigerator. My weight went up and down again forty pounds.

When Paul was busy, I worked with his colleague Cheryl. She too was a survivor and was a real comfort as I continued to pursue my healing. Cheryl often said to me, "*If God can heal me, God can heal you. He doesn't practice favoritism.*" (Galatians 2:6)

Cheryl seemed healthy, her faith was vibrant, and she was in her right mind. She was the only SRA survivor I had ever met who seemed to have been healed. Her testimony was an inspiration to me, and because of her I knew it was possible to recover.

Cheryl worked with me periodically, but when I got stuck she recommended I go see Henry, a farmer in southern Oregon. She said he had been very helpful facilitating her freedom, so I agreed to an appointment. When the day came, Cheryl drove me to the farm. I was a nervous wreck. My stomach hurt and everything inside me wanted to scream, "Turn the car around and take me home."

Noticing my distress Cheryl asked me how I was doing. I could barely spit out the words but I told her I was terrified. She reassured me that my feelings were understandable and very common, but they would soon pass.

Miles down the road we pulled into the gravel driveway of a modest farmhouse. I thought my heart would beat out of my chest. I simply didn't know what to expect.

We spent the day together. Cheryl prayed and Henry looked me right in the eye and asked questions. I was so uneasy I just wanted to jump out of my skin.

While sitting on the couch a memory suddenly surfaced. I was in France, in a huge castle with vineyards. My mother had dressed me up to meet the lady of the manor. Her name was Rothschild. She took me to her greenhouse where she had all kinds of unusual plants and several severed human heads. I was terrified of her. Rightly so, she seemed to think she owned me and could do with me as she pleased.

Next Henry called out a spirit by the name of Josef Mengele. In a flash I saw hundreds of images inside of a tall, slender, male figure with long black boots.

Henry said, "Mengele was a cult doctor who was so evil that he could have been called the Antichrist himself. He was known as "Dr. Death" at Auschwitz during World War II."

"What is he doing in me?" I exclaimed.

"He was obviously one of your perpetrators," replied Henry. "Mengele traveled extensively throughout the United States performing mind control on child victims, until his death in 1979." Henry further explained that the terrifying picture of Mengele in my mind was done with the use of mirrors to multiply the image and terrify the alters in my system, to keep them silent.

"It was likely done under hypnosis," Henry said.

"Henry," I asked. "Could this be where my fascination with holocaust stories started? I have been drawn to them since I was nine years old. I couldn't put down *The Diary of Anne Frank*. And even now Corrie ten Boom's *The Hiding Place* is one of my favorite books."

"Yes," he replied. "You suffered similar experiences. But their torture ended with the war, and yours has continued."

Some months later I visited Henry and his wife again, this time without Cheryl. Again I was anxious, but not nearly as apprehensive as I had been during the first visit. While sitting on the couch this time, I had a memory that looked like the inside of the White House. It could have been a mock replica, I don't know. I also remembered being trained to use a gun. Henry handed me a rifle, and with eerie clarity I knew just how to hold it. With this came the realization that I had been trained as an assassin.

I shared with Henry a memory I had recovered some years earlier that could have been the initial starting point for the assassin programming. The words "Kill or be killed" were emblazed in my mind when I was about three years old.

My father placed a huge knife in my hand and then placed his hands over mine. "Do it or die. Kill or be killed!" he demanded as he drove the blade into the chest of a victim.

I just stared at my blood-stained hands screaming "I didn't want to do it."

For days I washed my hands over and over again, because

I couldn't get the blood off. After the killing, I remember my family taunting me saying, "God will never forgive you. You are a murderer. You have committed the worst sin. God will never want anything to do with you. You are one of us now."

As a tiny little girl, I believed them.

It took me weeks to recover from the shock of that memory. Somehow I had gone from being the victim to the perpetrator in a matter of moments. The guilt and self-condemnation was suffocating. "If only I could have died instead…," I thought. I tried telling myself that it wasn't my fault, but that was little consolation. "They made me do it," I reasoned. But words didn't ease my pain.

Henry tried to reassure me that this was common. "Many of the SRA survivors I have worked with remember 'assignments' of this nature," he told me. "Why else would the government be involved? Mind control is done for the purpose of creating sleeper assassins, spies, and couriers. Under mind control they can create the perfect soldier, willing to do whatever is commanded with unquestioning precision."

I held the news of assassin training as a horrible, shameful secret that I couldn't tell anyone, probably because I couldn't forgive myself. But in 2004 that changed when I saw the movie *The Manchurian Candidate* on the big screen with my husband. The movie depicted mind control by government programmers and highlighted the training of an assassin. While seated in the theater with Carl I elbowed him and whispered loudly, "THIS IS FOR REAL!!!"

He replied, "Oh Kathy, don't be ridiculous, this is just a made-up Hollywood movie."

It is well-known that the Illuminati "hide in plain sight," often exposing their activities to the general public through use of movies, television, music, and other forms of media often deemed fiction. Inspired by the movie, I sought to discover more on the topic of mind control, the CIA, and the correlation with Josef Mengele.

I found some answers in the book titled *Bluebird; Deliberate Creation of Multiple Personality by Psychiatrists* written by Colin A. Ross, MD. The author researched over 15,000 pages of documents obtained from the CIA through the Freedom of Information Act. Dr. Ross describes in detail the CIA programs and experiments from the 1950s counter-intelligence work that ushered in an era of mind control and the deliberate creation of multiple personalities, now known as dissociative identities. The purpose for the CIA agenda was to create the perfect military weapon in the form of an amnesic mind-controlled slave, also known as a "Manchurian Candidate." In 1959 a book by the same name was written by Richard Condon and produced as a film in 1962 and rereleased again in 2004.

Under the code name "Operation Paperclip," the United States government secretly immigrated over 1600 Nazi scientists and personnel onto military bases across the country after the war, for the purposes of American scientific and military advancement. Was Josef Mengele among them?

Josef Mengele performed heinous and brutal medical experiments on thousands of prisoners of war at Auschwitz during World War II. He was particularly fascinated with twins. Ruthlessly he tortured and maimed thousands of people, and sent hundreds of thousands more to the gas chambers. He escaped Nazi Germany before the collapse of the Nazi party and went to Brazil via the Vatican. It is my belief that Josef Mengele shared his research with the CIA.

Through the use of hypnosis, LSD, and trauma, mind control isn't hard to achieve. One of the greatest lies perpetrated upon the general public by proponents of hypnosis is that people will *not* do something under hypnosis that violates their conscience.

In truth, people under the influence of hypnosis will kill without even remembering it.

What does the Vatican have in common with Freemasonry, NASA, CIA mind control, royal families, and Nazism? Could it be a conglomerate of superpowers that will one day constitute the New World Order? How better to manage a large population than through a percentage of mind-controlled slaves trained to perform on command like marionettes on a string.

Chapter 21

Bloodlines

During the first year of caring for my mother, I sorted through everything she owned. One of the unexpected treasures I found was a box of genealogical records and family letters. My mother had done years of meticulous research on her family line going back to 1754 when two brothers traveled to America by ship from Germany, with a Jewish surname. My mother never told me her ancestors were Jewish. Not once did it ever come up. The only obscure clue might have been the fact that she had plastic surgery done on her nose before I was born. She used to tease me about the size of mine, and now I have an inkling as to why.

Family letters described Masonic activity, especially at funerals, tracing back each of four generations to my great, great grandfather, the Secretary of La Petite Masonic Lodge in France. Of even more interest to me was a photograph with my mother, my aunt Virginia, and many of the members of her family proudly holding a large pentagram representing the Eastern Star, a Masonic fraternity for women. To become a member of the Eastern Star, each woman must be recommended by a Master Mason. Clearly, I could see friends and family, even extended family, all involved in Freemasonry, a Luciferian organization.

As I continued to dig through scrapbooks and photographs I found a full-page newspaper article with a picture of my great uncle, a celebrated 32nd degree Mason. He was also a renowned college professor who attempted to disprove the

Bible. But what intrigued me most were his journal notes of the civil war in Virginia and the trip he took to Egypt to help excavate the Sphinx.

I also found photographs taken by my mother from a recent trip to the Smithsonian Museum in Virginia. In my hand was the picture of a large painting created by my great uncle in 1896 of his excavation in Egypt. Near this point in the family history, the family name was changed by a single letter, changing it from a Jewish surname, to that known in demonology as the "Great Earl of Hell" and associated in Egyptian mythology with the sun god Ra.

In my later research into Freemasonry, I discovered Egyptian mythology and Egyptian witchcraft are key elements in Masonic rituals and the Rosicrucian Brotherhood to which I believed my ancestors belonged. As a child I remember my mother taking me to the Rosicrucian Egyptian Museum in San Jose, a place filled with Egyptian artifacts and founded by the Ancient Mystical Order Rosae Crucis. The Rosecrucian order is a fraternal Masonic-type organization, a secret society formed in seventeenth-century Germany.

My mother's generations didn't appear to come from royalty, but were most certainly tied to the occult in a powerful way. I've heard that witches don't marry beneath them when it comes to occult power. Marriages in the upper echelons of the occult are generally arranged both for power and to breed children for intelligence like one might breed race horses. My mother's occult bloodline joined the succession of my father's royal Stuart lineage to become a powerful alliance of occult capabilities, a certain distinction among Illuminati families.

I gathered this information as evidence, adding validity to my memories and insight into the generational lines from which I came. But I knew there was more. There had to be more.

CHAPTER 22

A New Millennium

We celebrated the New Year and the new millennium in downtown Portland. There was a huge crowd in the town square counting down the moments before the dawn of the next century. Marie was on her dad's shoulders and I was holding Bradley. There had been such fear and trepidation over this historic moment that many just held their breath as the clock struck midnight and firecrackers exploded over the river. It was a time of certain change.

After three years at Audio Visual View, I resigned and accepted a position at a large software company. They gave me a beautiful corner office, a fabulous salary, bonuses, and every possible amenity.

Carl was very pleased with my income in the new job and quickly replaced broken-down vehicles and began planning vacations. He helped me look after mom by frequenting the care home and ensuring her comfort. She referred to him affectionately as the "Candy Man" because he was known for bringing her chocolates when he visited.

On her seventy-sixth birthday, Carl and I brought her a cake and some small gifts during my lunch break. Her mind was clearly elsewhere, but she understood that we were celebrating her birthday.

Without warning she said, "Are the women coming to prepare me for the ritual? It's my birthday, I have to get ready."

My mouth fell to the table. Carl's big blue eyes were the size of saucers. For the first time a member of my family admitted to participating in satanic rituals. Carl could no longer deny it was real. I returned to the office in a state of shock. Every part of my body was numb.

When I came home from work Carl told me he stayed with mom for an hour that afternoon after I left. Then he looked at me and said, "It really is true. She said some of the things I've heard you say."

Rita's disclosure was one of many blessings and confirmations God gave me for being faithful to honor my mother, despite the horror of the past. Forgiveness came more easily with each passing year. I knew she too was a survivor, but never received healing. My heart softened until I could honestly say I loved her.

Surprisingly, I worked fewer hours with this new job and had more time for the family. Marie and Bradley continued to grow and mature. Marie was eleven years old and in that awkward stage between being a little girl and becoming a woman. Marie continued to do well in school but she was often lonely. Bradley was nine and every bit a boy. He lived and breathed skateboarding and did his very best to just slide by in school. Carl worked as a repair technician but managed to have time to drive the children to and from their activities. As the mundane set in, Carl lost interest in church and he began to backslide to his pre-baptism state. He stubbornly refused to discuss it with me.

I felt deeply concerned that the kids were following their father spiritually. There was nothing I could do but pray. Mama Jane prayed too. Whenever I needed her, she was there for me with love and prayer. I went to church every week without my husband and children, but Mama Jane was always there. After all of those years she still walked the aisles passing out her devotionals, though her lung condition had worsened and she had to carry an oxygen tank with her as she kissed and hugged everyone.

When Halloween loomed on the calendar in my office, I became uneasy. But for the company, this was a celebrated holiday. A contest for cubical decorating and best costume was scheduled as well as a huge potluck organized by human resources. I told the team they could decorate the department, but I had no intention of personally participating in the event. To my chagrin, the team decorated the entire area with a *Wizard of Oz* theme and the guys dressed as prostitutes while my secretary dressed as a pimp. I was embarrassed just looking at them. More than that, I was triggered.

I called Henry and described what was happening. He said, "Well Kathy, it sounds like you have *Wizard of OZ* programming."

"What's that?" I asked.

He explained that the cult often used stories like *Alice in Wonderland* or *The Wizard of Oz* to implant mind control programming, using alters as each of the characters in the story.

"Oh my word!" I exclaimed. "The only story I ever remember my father reading to me when I was a child was the *Wizard of Oz*. He bought me the entire series. In fact, I still have it in my garage."

Henry replied, "Every time you heard that story or saw the movie, it reinstated the programs. If you are ready, we can break it now."

I agreed. Henry spoke prayers over me to break the program, and then he called off all of the demons that had been layered into the program, over the phone. The demonic battle was fierce. Clutching the arms of the chair in front of me, I cried as Henry barked orders, commanding them out.

Shortly after Halloween, my boss called me into his office. He let me know that my employees were very upset that I had not participated in Halloween, and that the religious calendar in my office was offensive.

"You need to leave your religion at the door when you come to work," he said sternly.

I took a deep breath and replied, "Well sir, my beliefs and my God go with me wherever I go. It's not something I *can* leave at the door."

He received my reply graciously but I knew I was on shaky ground. When I thought about it I realized this was a strategic attack from the enemy to discredit me and steal my job. It felt like religious discrimination.

In November I asked to see the 2001 budget for my department. The division said corporate had it, and corporate said the division had it. As it turned out, neither had budgeted for my department. They finagled about one-third of the needed money to maintain a small team for the following year, but my salary was a large portion of that budget.

I called Mama Jane for advice. After praying about it she said, "Do not be unequally yoked together with unbelievers. For what fellowship has righteousness with lawlessness? And what communion has light with darkness?" (2 Corinthians 6:14)

I resigned, and worked through the last Friday of the year. Carl and the kids were upset with my decision. But pompously I said, "Oh, I can get another job in a heartbeat."

The perfect job didn't come in. Humbled and humiliated I was forced back into temporary employment.

In early spring that year Carl came home with his last paycheck, stating, "I've just been laid off." We both pumped out resumes while the state of Oregon competed with the state of Washington for the highest unemployment rates in the country.

I suggested we move, but Carl was steadfast. "No, I don't want to move the children. Moving would affect them as badly as it did Eddy and Lee when we moved to Colorado."

"Well, what do you propose we do?"

Carl answered, "We'll have to borrow some money from Rita's estate until we can both get back to work in decent jobs."

Reluctantly I agreed. Month after month we borrowed from the estate but there was no work in sight.

The attacks of September 11th still brings tears to my eyes, as I remember watching the news that morning. The economy continued to erode after the twin towers went down, and I knew I had to do something different. Realizing I could no longer compete in the labor market without a degree, I went back to school while working fulltime for a few dollars over minimum wage.

In the spring of 2002, we celebrated Carl's fiftieth birthday at the rehearsal dinner of our oldest son's wedding. Eddy married his high school sweetheart the next day in one of Portland's oldest churches. We bought Marie a beautiful gown and her first pair of high heels. She stole the camera in a floral headpiece that draped down her long brown hair. Her joy was absolutely contagious.

Bradley looked quite dapper in a beautiful blue shirt and the tuxedo he wore to usher in the guests. During the ceremony Eddy invited me up to the altar to light the "Mother's" candle, which deeply touched me. There was a very large wedding party assembled in the front of the church. Lee and his son Christopher, who was three at the time, stood near the bride and groom as they exchanged their vows. Carl and I were sitting attentively on the front pew when little Christopher, decked in a tiny tuxedo, squatted and said in his loudest voice, "I farted."

The audience erupted in laughter and thankfully so did the bride. I motioned with my finger, "Come to grandma, Christopher." But he was enjoying the attention too much to listen to me. Haley was a really good sport about it, until we threatened to do a family jig at the elegant reception to follow.

Carl struggled to find work for twenty-one months. I attended school full-time and worked temporary assignments intermittently for two years. Rita's money flowed out of her account like sand in a bag full of holes. In a panic I realized we were running out and could no longer afford the beautiful care facility we had her in.

I met with the facility director and explained our circumstances. She recommended an adult foster care home at half the price. We quickly moved mom into a foster care home. It wasn't fancy and there weren't any social activities, but by this time she had lost interest in those things anyway. I convinced myself it was the best thing to do.

Financial distress was hard on the whole family. The memories of poverty in Colorado and the bankruptcy just five years earlier were still fresh in our minds. Our kids were now in their early teens and began complaining about doing without. This season tried my faith but I held on to the belief that God would see us through. I just didn't understand why He was taking so long.

I was grateful that Carl and I didn't fight over money much. Instead we drew closer together to support each other and the kids through our challenges. We managed at times to just relax and enjoy the time off. We drove to the beach whenever the sun peaked through the gray Oregon skies and we took long bicycle rides around Sauvie's Island, weather permitting, and made love on the sandy banks of the Columbia River.

At Christmas our neighbors blessed us with enough food for a feast. And one of Marie's teachers, having heard of our plight, gave us enough money to buy presents for the entire family.

By 2003 I decided there had to be some other way to earn a living than answering phones for ten dollars an hour. If I couldn't get a management position, I decided to try for a sales job. I applied at a competitor to Audio Visual View in the education market. They hired me and put me in a tiny office suite with a single man. The position began with a salary and a twenty-five-mile drive across the river every day, for which I was determined to be grateful.

Carl went back to work just weeks after I did. By the time the first paycheck came in there was $100 left of Rita's estate. If God hadn't provided in this way, we would have lost our home and everything in it. We took care of mom and she took care of us. After all, I was the only surviving heir to the estate and it *was* my inheritance. However, I felt guilty for spending her money. Friends told me the estate was just compensating me for all of the years of therapy. The church told me I was committing elder abuse by using her funds and I should go to jail. Carl just said, "Kathy we will pay her back, a little at a time for as long as it takes." So we did.

The next time I went to visit mom I found her in the bathroom, combing the thin strands of white hair that slipped down along her forehead. As she turned to see me, her rubber soled shoes squeaked on the linoleum, sticky I presumed from dried urine on the floor. Her face lit up with excitement as though for a moment she recognized me.

She said, "I haven't seen you in such a long time."

I felt guilty. It had been a while since I had come to visit.

Then she looked intently into my eyes and asked with a smile, "How's your mother?"

I nearly choked before I replied, "Oh, I don't think she's doing so well."

Her eyes were softer than I had seen them in years. There was a childlike innocence about her smile that made me want to hold her and somehow make her world better. We sat for a moment. I held her hand.

Mom began to cry. "It's so good to see you," she said.

I left mom sitting at the dining room table in her pink

"Arizona" shirt. I couldn't look back as I reached for the door. It had been a very long five years. We had both changed. Maybe in some ways we were both softer around the edges, having been worn down by the constant stress of surviving the progression of Alzheimer's disease.

CHAPTER 23

Divine Networking

My office mate Charles and I hit it off really well. Sitting in that little office together all day, it was inevitable that we would get to know each other. I shared a bit of my story with Charles and he replied, "That is so interesting. God seems to be bringing SRA survivors into my life lately for some reason."

Charles was a deeply committed, mature Christian. From the start he taught me things about the Bible, prophesy, and spiritual gifts that I had never been exposed to before. He asked me if I had ever had any deliverance. I told him about the work I had done with Pastor Paul and Henry.

"What happened with that?" he asked.

"The family of an SRA survivor sued Paul's ministry and he stopped doing that type of counseling. Henry is a two hour drive from here."

Charles listened and then said, "If you really want some deliverance, you should drive up to Vancouver and meet the Solbergs."

I took his advice and made an appointment with Frank and Shirley Solberg. He was a retired pastor and his wife was his ministry partner. When I got to their door my stomach churned. Looking at my face Shirley asked if I was okay. I told her I felt terrible.

She took my arm, "That's the demonic trying to keep you from freedom. Come on in."

Each new minister the Lord brought me to for deliverance taught me something new. Frank and Shirley were no exception. They had discernment and were able to identify some of the demons tormenting me. However, they didn't forbid the demons from manifesting. By the end of an hour or two of ministry I was exhausted and soaked with sweat. Persistent however, I continued the work. At times Charles even came with me and battled on my behalf as well, until Frank passed away.

Day or night I was still plagued with fears, nightmares, and triggers. The same nightmare ran through my dreams with increasing frequency. I was always running for my life and hiding, afraid I would be found. Each time I had the dream, I woke just as I was caught. Sometimes the scenes were different, the faces different, but each time the theme was consistent. I assumed it was common for sexual abuse survivors. But as the dream occurred more frequently I began to suspect a memory. I mentioned it to my counselor. She didn't think it was a memory. She thought I just needed to express some feelings and accept my past. I realized it was time for a new counselor.

Upon recommendation, I decided to try a therapist in a remote college town forty-five minutes away. I was told she was skilled with eating disorders, trauma, sexual abuse, DID, and most importantly, she was a Christian. As a bonus she also used eye-movement desensitization and reprocessing (EMDR) with her clients.

I told Colleen it had been eight or nine years since I had done any work using EMDR, but that it was especially helpful for me. Colleen was warm and very kind. I felt I could trust her so I shared the recurring dream with her briefly. Almost instantly I was in the memory.

She asked me, "On a scale from one to ten, how high is your anxiety level?"

"It's a nine or ten," I replied, gasping. "I can hardly breathe I'm so frightened."

It's nighttime. I am naked and running. Faster, faster, I have to hide before someone sees me. I shot a glance behind me. Then I peered into a dark passageway looking for a place to hide. Terror propelled me. I was running for my life but I didn't know from whom. All I knew was if they found me I would die. Nothing looked familiar. It was a dirty little town. I didn't know where I was as I looked for a place to crouch down and hide. I turned to the left and a firm hand with a deep voice grabbed me.

"Oh my God," I thought. "I've been CAUGHT." The man struck me on the left side of my face. And I fell to the ground. Several men and a woman grabbed me and threw me into the back of a white van and sped away. I wanted to scream but there was a gag in my mouth. In the terror of the moment I gasped for breath.

Colleen asked, "Are you okay?"

I shook my head, then my lungs seized into a full-blown asthma attack while I dug in the bottom of my purse for my inhaler.

We waited a few minutes for the medication to work, and then proceeded with the EMDR. I couldn't see anything but I could hear them yelling in another language, probably Spanish or Portuguese. Then my body went limp. They had drugged me.

The memory seemed to span a great deal of time. I was awakened when a man opened the back of the van and pulled me out. Waves of nausea hit me, and I wretched on the ground. A man in military fatigues with dark greasy hair and a gun on his shoulder barked orders at me in a foreign language. But I knew what he meant. He held my arm tightly and we walked down a narrow dirt path surrounded by miles of pineapple fields stretching in all directions. I followed him, and others like him followed behind me. We walked until we arrived at a military camp. I recalled seeing a building with a sheet of metal draped across it. I was put in a tiny shack about the size of a chicken coop with a dirt floor. My hands and feet were tied. My shoulders ached and my body hurt all over while I remembered. Gunshots were fired. My ears were still ringing when Colleen suggested we stop there until the next session.

I sobbed all the way home. I knew something much worse was to come, but I didn't know what. Meanwhile I had to go on with my life, be a parent, get to work on time, and function as though this never happened.

That weekend we stayed at our neighbor's beach house as a family. The kids had a blast. Bradley and his best friend took boogie boards out on the waves, Carl eased into a lounge chair with a magazine, and I paced the floor.

On our last day there I decided to write in my journal.

When I was done Marie said, "Mom, you look so angry."

"I'm not angry honey," I replied. But I knew she was right. I wasn't hiding it very well. Beneath the surface a raging volcano was bubbling up from inside.

The following week I met with Colleen again. We went right into EMDR processing and more pictures splashed across my mind, resuming where we left off.

Now in the larger building with the metal roof, I was pressed against the wall where I could see shelves filled with hundreds of brown paper-like bricks. I suspect it was heroin.

Half a dozen or more men circled me like vultures. The men laughed and teased one another as each one raped me. When they were done, I was handed over to my mother.

"My mother? She was there?" I thought, incredulous.

When I complained she simply said, "This is your duty."

I felt as though I had been skinned alive, my feelings were so raw. That night I lay in bed alone, staring up at the ceiling. "Jesus, I need you. I need you so badly," I cried.

"I'm right here," He whispered. "Lay your head on my shoulder."

I imagined Him lying next to me, and I listened to His heart beat as I drifted off to sleep.

Chapter 24

Why God?

———⊥———

Certainly every person who has suffered from abuse at some point has to ask the question "Why God?" Then the inevitable follows, "If you really loved me, how could you let this happen?"

Just as Jacob wrestled with God in Genesis 32, I too wrestled with God over these questions.

"You knew if you gave me to those parents I would be ritually abused. Why did you send me God?" I implored. "How can I trust you to love and protect me *now* if you didn't do it then?"

> Psalm 139:16 says, *Your eyes saw my substance, being yet unformed. And in Your book they all were written, the days fashioned for me, when as yet there were none of them.*

"You knew the days of my life before I was born, God. Why did you put me in that womb?" I prayed. I didn't really expect an answer, when I heard the Holy Spirit reply, "Because I knew I could trust you."

"WHAT?" I exclaimed. "I don't get it. What do you mean you could trust me?"

There was no answer.

I was angry, "Where were you when this happened? If you really loved me you should have stepped in. You should have done something to stop it. If you are all powerful and in-control, why didn't you rescue me?"

"I did," He replied.

Then I remembered the sweet words of Pastor Paul, "You are a walking miracle."

I knew if I had a problem with God, the problem was on my side of the fence. But I needed answers to my sincere questions.

While driving to work one morning, listening to Christian radio, I heard a teaching that profoundly altered my perspective. I came to understand there are at least three different manifestations of God's will: His permissive will, His sovereign will, and His perfect will.

In God's permissive will He allows human beings to make their own choices. He is a gentleman and does not interfere with our free will. Why is free will so important? Because He wants us to freely choose to love Him. If He imposed it on us, it wouldn't be love. It wouldn't be free. So He gives us freedom to choose. We get to choose whether we will love Him and seek His perfect will for us, or we can choose to act as our human nature often demonstrates – in horrific wickedness.

Then I realized it wasn't God's will that I was abused. No, instead I believe He was crying right along with me. What pain it must have been for Him to see this evil perpetrated upon an innocent child.

Maybe it took tremendous restraint for Him not to come down from heaven to strike them all dead. Maybe it pained Him in the same way Jesus chose to stay on the cross, to suffer, and accomplish the Father's sovereign will.

When my parents abused me they were acting out of their sin nature. The same sin nature we all have, myself included. They chose to behave wickedly. They were exercising their free will. What they did was illegal. It was against God's moral law, and against His perfect will. But He gave them the right to choose and He didn't take that choice away until they breathed their last breath. The caveat is ... there are consequences to choices. The people who abused me had to live with their guilt and shame, and the damage to their relationship with God. Ultimately they will have to face Almighty God themselves on judgment day. God's word in Joshua 24:15 reads, *But if serving the Lord seems undesirable to you, then choose for yourselves this day who you will serve...* (NIV)

God's sovereign will is unchanging. The end of the story has already been written in the book of Revelation. Regardless of our choices, His sovereign will prevails. There is nothing you or I, or our parents, or even Satan can do to prevent the fulfillment of God's sovereign will.

God's perfect will is about abiding in Him. In His perfect will, His plans are manifested in and through our partnership with Him. In order for His best to manifest through our choices, we must choose to seek Him, love and obey Him, and whole-heartedly choose what He deems best. If we choose to walk in His will and His ways by seeking His heart regarding our choices, we will be walking in what His perfect will is for us. That doesn't mean it will be devoid of heartache or trials, but it will be for God's best and highest purposes. It is a place where we become clay in the potters hand, fashioned to become a vessel of honor, fit for use at the Master's table (2 Timothy 2:20-21).

I embraced the thought that God is always good. It is His nature, who He is. God is good. No work of the enemy can ever change that truth. Whether I believe it or not, the truth doesn't change. If God is good, then where do I place the blame?

Any little soul the Lord put in my mother's womb would suffer horrific abuse. But He knew He could trust me to come through and glorify Him. And maybe, I wondered ... did I actually choose the assignment? Maybe I said, "Papa God, send me. I'll survive. I'll persevere. I'll expose it and I'll glorify you." Somewhere deep in my spirit I wonder if that's what really happened.

In essence, I came to terms with the fact that God was there. He wouldn't violate his own law of free will, but He determined to provide every facet of His salvation in my life the moment I turned to Him. One of the Greek words for salvation is *Sozo* (Strong's 4982), which means to save, deliver and protect, heal, preserve, do well, and make whole. In every way God has worked His salvation through my life to make me, a multiple with thousands of parts, whole again. Being whole is a form of integrity, like a pitcher that does not leak, able to carry living water from the Master's table for the outpouring of His perfect will.

> *For I consider that the sufferings of this present time are not worthy to be compared with the glory which shall be revealed in us.* (Romans 8:18)

Chapter 25

Connections

Up the steps from the front door were bright yellow sticky notes that read "You can do it" and "I believe in you." I recognized Marie's handwriting. Now nearly fifteen years old, my daughter was my greatest encouragement. For two weeks I had been studying for my final exam in algebra, it was all that stood in the way of completing my bachelor's degree. Carl spent hours patiently going over algebra instructions with me, and finally this was the day of reckoning. I drove to the university and took the exam. While the computer calculated my score I held my breath. Squealing with elation, I hollered "I passed, I can't believe it! I passed."

I graduated from college with a new level of self-esteem and a Bachelor's Degree in Business Management. At thirty-nine years old, I wore a cap and gown for the first time. Carl and the kids cheered from the audience while I accepted my diploma. It felt like the greatest accomplishment of my life. Once and for all I wiped off the label "drop out."

Although I finally had a degree, management positions were still hard to find. I continued working in education sales, frequently complaining about the market and the lack of Oregon school funding. I felt stuck in a job where I wasn't successful, a marriage that was low on intimacy, and I had no idea where to go next for deliverance. Once again the Lord used Charles to divinely connect me.

He thought about it for a moment. "I know a guy in Wilsonville that you might like," Charles said. "If you don't mind the fact that he can really read your mail. He's very gifted. I saw him at a meeting recently and I was very impressed with him."

I called and made an appointment with Joseph, and on June 30th I arrived for our first meeting. I didn't know what to expect, but I was willing to do anything for healing.

It seemed with each new ministry and counselor God provided, He reached deeper and deeper down into the roots of my soul.

Counselors always had a list of case history questions that I dreaded When asked, "How long did the abuse continue?" I would usually say flippantly, "from birth to about twenty years of age." But deep inside I always suspected the abuse began before I was born. I didn't know how it happened or what had taken place. But I knew something significant and unexplored lay waiting in the depths of my heart. After nineteen years of therapy, five years in and out of 12-step meetings as well as four years of deliverance, I felt discouraged. "This is my last stop," I thought.

Along the way the Holy Spirit would whisper to me often, "Surrender it all to me, I don't waste pain. Whatever you give me I will use."

I recall feeling angry with God and retorting, "Then you have a lot of work to do to make something of forty years, years of nothing but pain. What is the purpose in this God? I don't understand," I confessed. "I'm still so desperate God."

Joseph and his wife Ruth were warm and loving. They were the grandparents I imagined but never had. I felt safe with them very quickly. We met in the dining room of their modest home so I could fill out paperwork. I expected the first appointment to be two hours of case history, but God had something else in mind. Joseph prayed and then said to me, "You have been horribly abused. I see a boat and you are a little girl, naked in a cage. The men are poking sticks at you and laughing."

I was speechless. How did he know that? Only God could have told him that. Joseph described this memory as though he had been there. Charles was right. This guy really could read my mail!

In this way, God confirmed to me that I could trust Joseph. He had an amazing gift to see and hear the guidance of the Holy Spirit. Joseph prayed over me and asked me to renounce the deep feelings of hatred toward the men who hurt me.

I agreed to do so.

Then he said, "Oh, you were rejected in the womb, and traumatized in a dedication to Satan."

There it was. A confirmation of that gut feeling that haunted me for years. My tears fell on the kitchen table. Then Joseph softly explained what the Holy Spirit had shown him.

He said, "Your soul split in two at birth. They traumatized you with your first breath into the world."

It felt like soul surgery. The Great Physician ministered to a pocket of deeply buried pain in my heart. As the emotional pain and grief oozed out of that wound, Joseph and Ruth prayed for God to heal me.

Joseph explained that the cry "Abba Father" in Greek is like the cry of an infant that has nothing but need (Romans 8:15-16 and Galatians 4:6). I doubled over, sobbing "Abba Father."

With that Joseph said, "Your Father in heaven has come to get His little girl. He has a new name for you. He calls you "Katie."

With their arms around me, Joseph and Ruth offered a prayer of dedication for the tiny infant parts of my soul to Jesus. They powerfully prayed, breaking the spiritual bondage from the satanic dedication. Ruth held me while I cried in her arms.

"Only God could have known what was there," I said. "Thank you so much. I am so grateful."

When I was able to compose myself again, I said, "I wondered what happened to me during those first few days in the world. My mother said she slept through labor, delivery, and then a couple of days after that. I must have been two or three days old before she held me for the first time." Wiping my eyes with a wad of Kleenex I said, "Well, this could explain why I never bonded with my mother."

Joseph replied, "There may have been more to it than that."

I recalled a recent therapy session I had with Colleen. She suspected a bonding disorder with me and explained how the disorder could cause a variety of problems, including compulsive overeating.

"I'm not a psychologist," Joseph said. "But I can remove the demons attached to this trauma at birth."

He said, "I see eighteen spirits of rejection operating in your life."

He bound them and commanded them out. His whole body shook as the anointing fell and the enemy fled. This ministry was painless, unlike any other I had experienced. There was no battle with the demons. They seemed to recognize his authority in Christ and left without resistance. Then Joseph asked me to embrace the parts of myself that had been fractured. These parts of me held the pain and the terror enabling me to survive. Joseph instructed the parts of my broken heart to give their pain and their memories to Jesus, and he read Psalm 147:2-7 to me.

> *The Lord builds up Jerusalem; He gathers together the outcasts of Israel. He heals the brokenhearted and binds up their wounds. He counts the number of the stars; He calls them all by name. Great is our Lord, and mighty in power; His understanding*

is infinite. The Lord lifts up the humble; He casts the wicked to the ground. Sing to the Lord with thanksgiving.

Joseph explained, "You see, Katie, God is building you up. He has named every broken piece of your heart and He gathers them all together to heal them. Only God can do these things."

I was so exhausted after this ministry session I went home and crawled into bed at 6:30 in the evening. I left that session with new eyes and a new perspective on myself. I felt compassion for my failings and understood that the deepest heart cry within me was that of an infant without words. This healing was so foundational to the essence of my being; I felt truly transformed.

Chapter 26

Divine Appointments

I scheduled subsequent ministry sessions with Joseph every few weeks. I looked forward to them as though my life depended on it. Joseph provided biblical teaching and Godly counsel for each of the areas in my life. We shared books and information as well as a deep love for the Lord. One afternoon I noticed a book on the coffee table when I came for ministry. I felt the Holy Spirit prompt me to pick up *Unmasking Freemasonry* by Selwyn Stevens. On the cover I recognized the strange diamond shaped symbol from the walls and doorways of the dark building my mother used to take me to. "Hey Joseph, can I borrow this book?"

"Sure," he replied.

When I returned for the next session I asked Joseph if we could do the Freemasonry renunciations contained inside. It took us three sessions to get through each of the Masonic degrees and to renounce and break each of the curses. We tediously combed through generations of Freemasonry and Illuminati curses in my family line, with the guidance of the Holy Spirit. When we were finished, we kicked out spirits of asthma, infirmity, sickness, and fear, along with a menagerie of others. I felt physically lighter after each session.

Several days after we finished the last of the Freemasonry renunciations I realized I had not used my asthma inhaler. I was able to reduce the oral medication until I stopped taking it completely, with no recurring asthma symptoms. Enthusiastically I realized God had healed my lungs. For the first time in nearly forty years I was free of asthma medication. With that I dedicated every breath in my body to Almighty God for His glory.

When I told Joseph he said, "Remember this Katie, the healing doesn't come when there is a curse in place. We broke the curses of Freemasonry, kicked out the demons, and the healing came. Praise God."

1 John 1:2 reads, *Beloved, I pray that you may prosper in all things and be in health even as your soul prospers.* It seemed the healing also came as my soul healed.

In August I asked Joseph to minister around my addiction to sugar and compulsive overeating.

He said, "Katie there is so much important work to do here I'd prefer to do first, but I know this is a daily issue for you. Okay," he paused, "we will proceed in faith in that direction."

Joseph called forth every part of my broken heart that was addicted to sugar. He laughed, "Katie you aren't overeating, you're eating for twenty. There were twenty alters inside you who were addicted to sugar and compulsive overeating."

He kicked out demons of sugar addiction from my abuse of tobacco, alcohol, and food. He bound every demon of addiction, anorexia, bulimia, and compulsive overeating. Then he invited all of these alters to receive their healing in Jesus and to integrate back into my soul. The difference was absolutely remarkable. I was able to abstain from unhealthy eating for the first time in my life. It marked the beginning of a yearlong abstinence from food addiction wherein I lost thirty-seven pounds without dieting, starving, binging, or purging.

The healing journey was very cyclical for me. One session would end on a high note and the next would beckon the work into deeper and more challenging layers. After a couple months of working with Joseph, I mentioned that more child alters in me were agitated and upset, making it difficult to function. We began our session with prayer and then the Holy Spirit gave Joseph the name "Hannah" and he called her forward. She was the spokesperson for dozens of broken child pieces inside. As Joseph ministered to her, all of the little alters with her came forward for healing. They laid their memories and their pain at the feet of Jesus and He miraculously healed them and they integrated instantly.

Each ministry session I had with Joseph was helpful. But I still struggled daily to function with so many hurting pieces inside. I prayed in the car on the way to the following meeting. "God, I need another miracle. I want to be whole. Please help me."

When I arrived at Joseph and Ruth's home for ministry, the Holy Spirit whispered to Joseph, "Katie is going to do a 360 today." Joseph assumed it meant a complete turnaround.

At the start of the session I said, "After all of the years of therapy and deliverance, I am getting weary of the daily battle just to get well. I know we've made progress, but I need more than that. I just want to be healed." Tears rolled down my cheeks.

Joseph took a deep breath. "Okay Katie, put your faith in a miracle today. Let's see what God's going to do."

Joseph began calling alters in groups by age or circumstance to Jesus. As each group received healing, Joseph wrote down the number of alters integrated. We'd been working steadily for a couple of hours when I could suddenly feel contractions. One after another they came and I realized it was another baby memory. The alter carrying the memory came forward with details. I was seventeen in the memory and again my child was sacrificed to Satan. I moaned in pain and grieved from the very core of my soul. Ruth held me and I sobbed uncontrollably for half an hour.

Then Joseph said, "Are you ready to heal this? You don't have to sit in the pain Katie; it's time for God to heal and integrate her."

Like a rock, the alter dropped the memory, with all of the grief and pain, at the feet of Jesus. Jesus took her in His arms and she received her healing. It took me a moment to comprehend the gravity of my loss. This was child number four snatched from my womb by the dragon.

Softly Joseph said, "I see four little children in heaven Katie, waving down at you. Three are little boys and one little girl. They are with Jesus, Katie. And when Jesus takes you home they will all be there to see you. They are just fine, and they love you so much."

The Holy Spirit ministered deeply in my heart, comforting and healing the deep gash in my soul by knitting it back together with love and precision.

I thought for a moment and said to Joseph and Ruth, "This must have been the birth the doctor at Stanford asked about when I was seventeen," I said. "It makes sense now. No wonder my father was so nervous about those doctor appointments. He asked me so many questions about them."

My mother came to mind. When I was a child she told me that she had eight miscarriages before I was born. It made me wonder what she had been through.

After three and one-half hours of ministry we finally wrapped up the session. Joseph counted the number of alters we integrated and declared "Katie we integrated 360 alters today. I've never seen the Lord do that many in one session before. It's a miracle." He said, "This is your complete turn-around Katie. God is now going to release you to minister to others."

When I got home my husband didn't even notice anything different about me. But I did. My head was quiet, my soul was at peace, and my spirit was on fire for God. I told Carl that God had done an amazing healing in me. To which he replied, "Oh, that's nice honey."

In mid-September I met with Joseph again. We had our plan for the ministry time laid out on paper, but when Joseph began to speak, there was an outpouring of his prophetic gifting. He described each vision as the Lord revealed them.

He smiled broadly and said, "There is an angel with us and he keeps tapping me on the shoulder to continue. I don't think we are going to get to this list today Katie. God has something else in mind."

We recorded it all on tape. When transcribed, it filled twenty-one pages of typed text. In the message was the clear herald to write the book you are reading today. It was the launch pad for the dreams placed in my heart as a child and a word of hope for my future.

"Joseph," I said, "I would love to minister to others if I had an anointing like yours and could hear God the way you do."

Joseph smiled, "Katie, God has already put those gifts in you."

"He has? I always knew my calling was to help other survivors, but I thought I needed a master's degree to do that."

Laughing Joseph said, "People with degrees come here and ask me how their clients are getting well so rapidly. I just tell them it is the Holy Spirit."

I was so moved by the content of that session that I floated on a cloud for days. Everything Joseph prophesied lined up with the desires of my heart. God spoke through Joseph the future He laid on my heart when I was a little girl. I couldn't stop crying, it was the core message of my life and calling, the reason I survived.

I continued to see Joseph and Ruth for ministry once a month for a while. They became my spiritual parents and my mentors. When I came for ministry, I could ease into their couch, and soak in the peace and love. It was my home away from home.

They ministered around my marriage issues, concerns about my teenagers, and continued to help me through deliverance, healing, and integration. I grew stronger emotionally, spiritually, and physically with each session.

It was about this time that Joseph asked me if I would like to become part of his ministry team.

"Really?" I exclaimed.

"Yes," Joseph replied seriously. "I have prayed about this and I feel the Lord has asked me to make this invitation to you."

Elated, I asked what it would involve.

"We would ordain you as a pastor, train you, provide prayer covering for you, and you would be released to minister to others."

"Like you have ministered to me?" I asked.

"Exactly," said Joseph. "We consider ordination a marriage to the call God has placed upon your life."

Joseph and Ruth made arrangements to ordain me during a New Year's Eve celebration. I invited a Christian friend from Audio Visual View as well as my husband and children. But Carl and the kids chose not to come.

I was nervous and didn't know what to expect. Many spiritually gifted and powerful people of God were there when I arrived with my friend, most of whom I met for the first time that night.

A man at the party called me "Mary" and then smiled.

"You are blessed among women," he said.

Then I remembered the way the Lord had said he could trust me. They prayed and laid hands on me as described in Acts 13:2-3, and my life changed forever.

This was just the beginning of a life surrendered to serve. When Joseph was invited to the coast to minister and then to southern Oregon, he graciously invited me to go with him and his wife.

Joseph would say, "Katie, you go over there and pray for those people, and I'll pray for these."

I felt like I had been pushed into the deep end of the pool without knowing how to swim. But the Holy Spirit was faithful to lead me from glory to glory, every step of the way.

"The place God calls you to is where your deep gladness and the world's deep hunger meet."
- Frederic Buechnerr

Chapter 27

More to Remember

In April 2005, I received a phone call from Jane's family letting me know she was in intensive care. At some time during the night she had stopped getting oxygen. I rushed to the hospital to find her unconscious, tied to various hoses and wires. It broke my heart to see her that way. The only thing I could think to do was sing her favorite song, "What a Friend We Have in Jesus." Two days later she went to be with her beloved Savior.

Jane's family made arrangements to hold her memorial at the church, and her daughter asked me to say a few words in her memory.

The day of the memorial Carl and the kids dressed up to attend her service. Jane had become an important member of our family and we all loved her.

At the entrance to the sanctuary Carl, Marie, and Bradley helped to hand out programs. It was then I noticed on the back of the program was the poem "Rose Sweet" that Mama Jane had given to me ten years earlier. It had been reproduced as a celebration of her devotionals. Of all the poems she wrote, her daughter chose that one for the program. When I stood up to speak, I unfolded the copy of Jane's poem from my Bible. The color had faded and the paper was worn. But it meant more to me at that moment than words could say.

It was my privilege to honor her. I shared with the audience how Jane blessed us from the moment we met her in the grocery store, how she prayed to save our marriage, and how she helped to reconcile me with my biological mother. There wasn't a dry eye in the house. To this day, I still miss Mama Jane. But I have no doubt heaven is a brighter place because she is there with Jesus.

Rose Sweet

A thornless Rose came to the earth,
our sin and guilt to bear.
He was just a tiny bud at birth,
Yet His fragrance filled the air.
He bloomed and grew in love and grace,
He touched, He taught, He fed.
He gave of Himself, not counting the cost.
He did what His Father said.
What brought that Blossom to full bloom
was a crown of thorns and a tree.
The pain deeply pierced our Tender Rose,
As He gave His all for you and for me.

Father dear; we're strange creatures, rejecting realities we can't grasp, though some ultimately cost us death over life. Creator, You understood and compassionately gave us the gift of faith in order to draw us back to You. Faith doesn't require we understand it all. Faith enables us to respond to Your call for us... to trust You Father, through Jesus Christ; and to acknowledge our sin of wanting independence from You. To live by our faith is to come to see the reality of You and the gift of eternal life both now and throughout eternity.

Dear one, if you have never, by faith, asked Jesus into your heart, won't you today? If you confess with your mouth 'Jesus is Lord' and believe in your heart that God raised him from the dead, you will be saved (Romans 10:9-10). Won't you become one of God's children today?

– Let your faith live. Reprinted by permission.

Although I had been released by God into ministry and I was walking in tremendous healing, there was still more to remember. Unlike years before when the memories flooded in, now they came sporadically, as unwelcome guests in my life.

One very vivid memory was of Josef Mengele. I could clearly see him on the airport tarmac, having just exited from a small plane.

He said to me, "I know your father."

I remembered that my father spoke German, and fondly described his love for the German people and their food. He was a Navy pilot in World War II in Germany. Was he a double agent? I don't know.

In the next scene, Mengele drove me to his home in a beautiful car. He handed me over to his maid, who promptly directed me upstairs to change my clothes. I was dressed in a beautiful deep blue velvet gown and invited to sit at an ornately set table. A royal couple sat across from me. The man wore a red sash with a Teutonic cross, and the woman was dripping in diamonds. Servants attended us with white gloves and all I could think was "don't spill the milk."

When the dishes were cleared, a severed human head with long blonde hair was dropped on the table in front of me. I let out a bloodcurdling scream. My head was then slammed to the table and my blonde hair parted to expose my neck – the threat was clear; "you talk, you die." A séance followed and then a killing. In eerie clarity I remembered taking marriage vows to Mengele in his living room.

There were other memories related to Nazism too. I recalled an isolated military outpost, men in green wool uniforms, and long black boots. I was forced to watch black and white movies of World War II concentration camps, and left in a cold dark cell without food or water. The message was, "be loyal to us and this won't happen to you." Later I discovered this was the formation of concentration camp programming, preparation for the end-times establishment of the New World Order.

There was even a memory that occurred in my late teens. I was taken in a military helicopter to a place near San Francisco where I was subjected to water boarding for talking.

"Who did you tell?" the voice demanded.

Gasping and terrified, I screamed "No one."

"AGAIN," the voice commanded, and my head was thrust in the cold water.

"NO," I screamed. "I won't talk. I won't tell anyone."

"AGAIN," I heard as I coughed and gagged on the water, fully expecting to drown.

I don't know how long the torture lasted, but it left an indelible imprint on my soul.

More horrific were my memories of satanic rituals at the Vatican. There were two of them. In the first I saw a gold cage that led me into a deep dark place underground. I was naked and tied to a dark stone altar. The room was bone-chilling cold and made the hair on my body stand on end. A stream of men in hooded robes entered the room with candles, chanting. It sounded like the Gregorian chant I studied in middle school. The sound reverberated off of the stone walls and went right through me. My heart was pounding. I recognized the word "Christi" spoken in Latin. Terrified, I concluded that I was the sacrifice. A pentagram was drawn on my torso in blood and I heard the words "No talk! No talk!" I knew the man with the red shoes was the pope and I feared for my life as he sexually abused me.

He said, "You are mine now. You belong to me."

There was talk of a baby and the seed of Satan. Then he commanded me to worship him.

"No," I screamed.

A sharp curved knife was pressed against my throat. "Do it!"

In a subsequent memory I gave birth again, on that same table in that horribly cold and deathly place. Screaming in terror in my own voice I heard, "Oh my God. I can't do it. No, I can't. I don't want to. You can't make me."

Another voice said, "Who do you think you are? You little wretch. This is my decision. No one can help you now. Give me the baby."

"NO."

"Give me the baby," he demanded.

"You horrible man," I screamed. "You are disgusting."

He smacked me hard. "It's all a charade isn't it?" He cackled. "You're such a good little girl, aren't you?" he mocked.

Then he turned his attention toward the baby. "My son," he said in a calculating tone. Then he slit the baby's throat and proceeded with the ritual.

I didn't care anymore. And for that I felt guilty. I didn't want his baby and I didn't want to grieve for its loss. In total, Satan killed five of my babies.

Blessed are those who mourn, for they shall be comforted. (Matthew 5:4)

Chapter 28

Darkest Before the Dawn

Carl and I celebrated our eighteenth anniversary at an elegant restaurant. Our marriage was a mess, and it grieved me to sit there and pretend all was well. After nearly ten years of sobriety I ordered a glass of wine. It was my way of shaking my fist at God.

Just two months later, on a rainy cold evening before Christmas 2006, I left Carl and moved into my own apartment a couple of miles down the street. It was a mutual decision that ripped our family apart.

Bradley, then sixteen, offered to stay with me to keep me company, but the apartment wasn't really home for him. Part of the family conflict involved problems between Marie and me as well. Marie stayed with her father and only visited occasionally.

I had a job as the Administrator of a church in the area, which occupied my hours. And I was able to provide prayer ministry in my spare time, still under the tutelage of Joseph and Ruth. But a month after my separation from Carl, the church let me go. I felt like I lost two families in a single blow. From there I tumbled into a deep depression.

In April my mother died. It was the end of more than eight long years of watching her agonizing decline. I wondered if it was a relief for her to leave her earth suit behind. Over and over again the Lord reassured my troubled heart that she was with Him, and she was finally free in heaven.

Carl and I drove to the beach with her ashes. At sunset, we carefully opened the box and cut open the bag that contained her remains. It didn't seem real. This was all that was left of her. Gently we poured her ashes into the Pacific Ocean and I watched as the current washed her away.

Grief assailed me like a rabid dog. My guts were mangled in chronic bowel pain. I couldn't work, let alone drive, and I had to close my tiny ministry office. Six months after the separation, nothing had changed between Carl and me. He wasn't willing to attend marriage counseling, and the same issues remained unresolved. He admitted his "salvation" was just a rouse to keep the family together. With the children nearly grown it was no longer necessary to keep up the charade.

Carl went so far as to call my oldest brother in California. "The only thing your brother told me was that your mother used to call you an evil child," Carl said.

I was furious, "After seventeen years without contact you took it upon yourself to call him? What gave you the right to do that? Did you also tell them where we live?"

"I just needed to know for myself if what you remembered was real," he replied.

"Couldn't you just take my word for it?" I yelled.

Not two weeks later Carl brought me a binder he had borrowed from a local Christian university about False Memory Syndrome. He was somehow hoping a denial of my past would restore our marriage. I was so furious I never wanted to speak to him again.

I took the matter to the Lord in prayer and I asked Him for permission to divorce my husband. His answer was a firm "no."

With that I lost my will to live. From day to day I just existed, slipping deeper and deeper into a bottomless pit of despair.

Antidepressants, therapists, and psychiatrists couldn't help me. I had come to the end of myself.

In June Marie graduated from high school, and on Father's Day she moved into her own apartment, leaving Carl and Bradley alone in that big empty house. I missed them terribly. Our lives were in ruins and it seemed there was nothing I could do about it.

My friend Sarah called, worried about me. "Hey, would you like to go to Bend with me for a couple of days?" she suggested.

"I don't know. I don't feel up to doing anything," I replied.

But Sarah insisted. She picked me up the following weekend and we drove for three hours to central Oregon. We attended a church service with a special guest speaker traveling from out of state. To my surprise I was pulled out of the crowd and ministered to personally in front of everyone. A powerful woman of God, this minister commanded the spirit of depression to break off of me. It was like my soul was suddenly uncorked and I wailed in front of the whole congregation, snot running down my face and all.

Then the minister began to sing, "Jesus loves me this I know because the Bible tells me so…" She looked me in the eyes and said gently, "You don't believe that Jesus really loves you, do you?"

Shaking my head, I couldn't stop crying.

"Well, He does love you. Regardless of your circumstances you need to know that Jesus will never stop loving you. Your prescription is to sing this song every day. I want you to sing it with all of your heart and believe it. Jesus does love you."

That was the breakthrough I needed. I took her advice and sang that song several times a day, every day until the depression lifted. Then I took an old coffee can and wrote the words "God Can" on it. Inside I placed a list of everything I needed from Him, from a physical healing, to a job and the restoration of my family. By faith I decided to trust in Him again.

If there was anything I learned from this experience, it was to keep my eyes on Jesus, regardless of my circumstances. Somehow in the back of my mind I had believed the lie that if Jesus loved me He wouldn't have let these things happen. It was a crazy way of thinking, but I believed that God was punishing me for an unknown crime and my life wasn't worth living. But when I renounced all of that and embraced the truth of His love, my circumstances began to turn around.

Within a month I was back to work as a temporary employee and slowly I was able to accept new clients for ministry. I signed another lease for the apartment and settled into my new life alone. I saw my children from time to time, but realized they had grown up and didn't need me much anymore.

In September I took a long walk during my lunch break in downtown Portland. It was a beautiful autumn day with a gentle breeze blowing colorful leaves of orange and brown around my feet. As I walked I talked to Jesus as though He was walking right along beside me. My mind traveled to the book of Nehemiah and I tried to imagine what it looked like when he was commissioned by God to repair the broken down walls of Jerusalem. It was idolatry that took down those walls and a calling from God that restored them. Then a thought occurred to me. People choose to allow God to restore their lives. It isn't an accident, it's a choice. The gates around the city represent the will – what we let in, and what we keep out. At that precise moment God gave me a vision for a whole new ministry.

I delighted in the idea that someday I could fully engage in ministry again. But I held the vision loosely, because like everything else in my life it hurt when the Lord had to pull my tightly controlling fingers off of it.

Looking back I could see so many times when I refused to trust God. I wouldn't surrender. I had to be in control. But He loved me anyway and He waited. When the storms of life came,

I screamed at God and shook my fist, clinging to my earthly understanding. "Your watch is broken God," I would yell. "You promised you'd fix this and you haven't."

"Trust me more," He would whisper in my ear. "I'm here. Trust me."

In my tantrum, I would stomp my feet. "No, I can't trust you – you'll abandon me. I'm going to do it my way!"

It was as though my Heavenly Father would smile at His toddler and say, "Okay, but when you are ready, I'm here."

With all of my might I would pound my forehead against life's wall of circumstances. When I could fight no more, I would crawl up into the lap of my Papa God and say, "I can't do it."

"I know. This is just too big for you," He would say, "But I can make it better. Will you let me?"

Hope grew in my heart and I believed my life had purpose again. My health improved, my ability to function improved, and I enjoyed an intimate relationship with God. I poured over His word, believing every chapter was a love letter from His heart to mine. All I wanted to do was serve Him in obedience.

When it was time to write my rent check for November I heard the Holy Spirit very clearly say, "Give your notice on the apartment."

"What?" I thought. I had just renewed the lease and I was finally happy living alone.

"Call Carl and tell him you want to come home," I heard the Holy Spirit say.

Was this my imagination? I chewed on the idea for a few minutes. Nothing had really changed between Carl and me. He still didn't believe in ritual abuse, he wasn't walking with the Lord, he wasn't in favor of ministry, and he was unwilling to go to counseling with me or even for himself. We weren't close. Two-thirds of my life involved topics Carl didn't want to hear about. Respectfully I asked, "Lord if this is really from you, would you please confirm it?"

The next day I was invited to lunch by a friend who was entertaining a prophetess from Seattle. "Join us," she said. "I want you to meet Carla."

Over warm biscuits and salad Carla confirmed what the Lord had spoken to me.

Reluctantly I followed His instructions and in a giant leap of faith I called Carl. He agreed to give our marriage another chance, on the condition that I didn't do ministry at home. "If you want to minister to people, please do it somewhere else," he said.

I agreed, and plans were made for a move home before Thanksgiving. Carl painted the spare bedroom for me and cleaned the house. Once home, the chronic bowel distress completely disappeared. It wasn't easy to reintegrate in the home. As a matter of fact, it was bumpy at first. I had changed, Carl had changed, and we couldn't take anything for granted. But after all those trials and tears, we still loved each other. I knew the only way this marriage had a chance was if I continued to seek the Lord for His instructions and was obedient to the prompting of His Spirit. I felt Him instruct me to love and accept Carl precisely as he is. Not to try to change him or convince him of something he can't fathom, but to just love him unconditionally. It didn't happen overnight, but slowly Carl and I drew closer together.

At the time of this writing, Carl and I have just celebrated our twenty-fifth wedding anniversary, loving each other more today than on the day we married. God is still in the miracle-working business.

Chapter 29

A Purpose for the Pain

What possessed Almighty God to reach down from heaven and pull an angry and rebellious woman from the clutches of Satanism? It had to be love.

For I am persuaded that neither death nor life, nor angels, nor principalities nor powers, nor things present nor things to come, nor height nor depth, nor any other created thing, shall be able to separate us from the love of God which is in Christ Jesus our Lord. (Romans 8:38-39)

Of all my generations, God chose to break the cycle of multigenerational Satanism with me.

The Scripture says, *You did not choose Me, but I chose you and appointed you that you should go and bear fruit and that your fruit should remain...* (John 15:16)

This is my heart cry today, "Lord, make my life fruitful for your kingdom."

One of the greatest gifts to come out of the crucible of pain was an intimate dependence on God and the sustenance of His Word.

"Katie," He would say, "I won't waste the pain. Give it to me."

The tapestry of my life was a mess of knots and strings, but the Master Craftsman created something beautiful in His time. *And we know that all things work together for good to those who love God, to those who are the called according to His purpose.* (Romans 8:28)

My life's most defining moment happened in Israel in 2008. I was traveling with an intercessory prayer team commissioned to pray over the walls of Jerusalem and throughout the region as Gideon's Army.

On our first day we went to the Valley of Armageddon and stood at the symbolic "gates of hell," the ruins of Megiddo.

The rabbi said, "It is here we must come against the fear of the future."

My mind flashed to the Omega programming in me that was intended to go into effect with the New World Order and the great battle of Armageddon (see Revelation 16:14, 16). I stood at the gate overlooking the valley weeping. All of the plans of my generations and all of the programming to ensure a victory for evil had come to nothing because I stood there for Jesus Christ.

> *Blessed be the God and Father of our Lord Jesus Christ, the Father of all mercies and God of all comfort, who comforts us in all our tribulation, that we may be able to comfort those who are in any trouble, with the comfort with which we ourselves are comforted by God.* (2 Corinthians 1:3-4)

If I were to offer any advice to fellow SRA survivors, I would say, "If He can heal me, He can certainly heal you. I don't believe it is possible to really heal outside of relationship with Jesus. If you have been abused by someone claiming to be Jesus, I urge you once again to seek the one true and living God. Regardless of the wreckage, God loves you and will heal you if you let Him. Who you are is not determined by what happened to you – the important matter is whose you are.

In these end-times, witchcraft is rampant in our culture. It isn't just fun and games, or even fantasy. If my story does nothing else, I pray it is an eye-opener to the public, that evil is real and dangerous. And the only power of victory over darkness is Jesus Christ.

Come out from among them and be separate, says the Lord. Do not touch what is unclean, and I will receive you. (2 Corinthians 6:17)

How do you desensitize a Christian nation to participate in witchcraft? You make it seem harmless like the classic TV show *Bewitched* or put *Harry Potter* books (that instruct children to conduct spells) on every school library shelf in the nation. Maybe even dress your children up to celebrate Halloween by tricking demons and giving out treats on a satanic holiday. Portland is known for VooDoo Donuts and even a Christian radio station identifies with it. *Woe to those who call evil good and good evil; who put darkness for light, and light for darkness.* (Isaiah 5:20)

1 John 4:4 says, *You are of God, little children, and have overcome them, because He who is in you is greater than he who is in the world.*

It took the power of Jesus to mend my broken heart, deliver me from evil, and restore my soul (Isaiah 61:1-3). Only Jesus could do that. He gave me beauty for ashes, the oil of joy for mourning, the garment of praise for the spirit of heaviness.

And He said, "Instead of your shame, you shall have double honor." (Isaiah 61:7)

In these last days it is critical that SRA survivors find their hope and healing in Christ. The programming must be broken to proclaim liberty to the captives and the opening of the prison to those who are bound (Isaiah 61:1).

To this end I have dedicated my life.

And they overcame him by the blood of the Lamb and by the word of their testimony, and they did not love their lives to the death. (Revelation 12:11)

About the Author

Katie has a passion to see the broken hearted healed, and set free. She is an ordained minister with a Masters of Christian Counseling degree from Christian Leadership University. She is the founder and pastor of a church and ministry providing Biblical counseling, inner healing, and deliverance ministry to severe trauma survivors.

Connect with Katie
www.revelationgateway.com
contact@revelationgateway.com

Made in the USA
San Bernardino, CA
27 April 2016